PHILOSOPHICAL ADVENTURES

PHILOSOPHICAL ADVENTURES

Steven M. Cahn

broadview press

BROADVIEW PRESS – www.broadviewpress.com
Peterborough, Ontario, Canada

Founded in 1985, Broadview Press remains a wholly independent publishing house. Broadview's focus is on academic publishing; our titles are accessible to university and college students as well as scholars and general readers. With over 600 titles in print, Broadview has become a leading international publisher in the humanities, with world-wide distribution. Broadview is committed to environmentally responsible publishing and fair business practices.

Library and Archives Canada Cataloguing in Publication

Title: Philosophical adventures / Steven M. Cahn.
Names: Cahn, Steven M., author.
Description: Includes bibliographical references and index.
Identifiers: Canadiana (print) 20190126981 | Canadiana (ebook) 2019012699X | ISBN 9781554814763 (softcover) | ISBN 9781460406717 (HTML) | ISBN 9781770487154 (PDF)
Subjects: LCSH: Philosophy—Introductions.
Classification: LCC BD21 .C34 2019 | DDC 100—dc23

Broadview Press handles its own distribution in North America:
PO Box 1243, Peterborough, Ontario K9J 7H5, Canada
555 Riverwalk Parkway, Tonawanda, NY 14150, USA
Tel: (705) 743-8990; Fax: (705) 743-8353
email: customerservice@broadviewpress.com

Distribution is handled by Eurospan Group in the UK, Europe, Central Asia, Middle East, Africa, India, Southeast Asia, Central America, South America, and the Caribbean. Distribution is handled by Footprint Books in Australia and New Zealand.

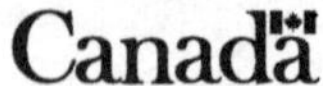

Broadview Press acknowledges the financial support of the Government of Canada for our publishing activities.

Edited by Robert M. Martin
Book Design by Em Dash Design

PRINTED IN CANADA

To my wife,
Marilyn Ross, MD

Contents

Preface

Philosophy is a subject unlike any other. No formulas need be memorized, no field work is necessary, and no equipment is required. The only prerequisite is an inquiring mind.

The word *philosophy* is of Greek origin and literally means "the love of wisdom." But what sort of wisdom do philosophers love?

The clearest answer may be found by exploring specific philosophical problems, but as a start we can say that philosophers seek to apply reason to the most fundamental questions, including: Do human beings ever act freely? Does God exist? Is morality based on fact? What ways of living are best? Which form of government is preferable? Should all education be vocational?

Yet these matters, which have been of special concern to me, are but a sample of the range of philosophical issues, including the nature of reality, knowledge, mind, meaning, justice, and beauty. No single volume can cover them all in detail, so here I shall concentrate on those that have not only been my focus but also have proved effective in conveying to others the spirit of philosophical inquiry.

I have drawn in part on my previously published books and articles but have reworked the material to provide a unified presentation. Here are my sources:

A New Introduction to Philosophy. Harper & Row, 1971. Reprinted by Wipf and Stock Publishers, 2004.

Puzzles & Perplexities. Second Edition. Lexington Books, 2007.

"The Altruism Puzzle," *Journal of Social Philosophy*, Vol. XLIV, No. 2 (Summer 2013).

"The Bus Puzzle," *Teaching Ethics*, Vol. 15, No. 2 (Fall 2015).

Happiness and Goodness: Philosophical Reflections on Living Well (with Christine Vitrano). Columbia University Press. 2015.

Religion Within Reason. Columbia University Press, 2017.

Teaching Philosophy: A Guide. Routledge, 2018.

Exploring Philosophy: An Introductory Anthology. Sixth Edition. Oxford University Press, 2018.

Inside Academia: Professors, Politics, and Policies. Rutgers University Press, 2019.

The Road Traveled and Other Essays. Wipf and Stock Publishers, 2019.

I wish to express my appreciation to Stephen Latta, my editor at Broadview Press, for his support and guidance, and to philosopher Robert M. Martin for his insightful comments. I also thank my brother, Victor L. Cahn, Professor Emeritus of English at Skidmore College, for innumerable stylistic and substantive suggestions. To my wife, Marilyn Ross, MD, I owe more than I would try to express in words.

PART I: REASONING

1 The Elements of Argument

Because philosophy calls for us to be reasonable, the question immediately arises: What is reason? The answer is found in this opening chapter, an earlier version of which I co-authored with Patricia Kitcher, now Professor of Philosophy at Columbia University, and George Sher, now Professor of Philosophy at Rice University. At one time we were colleagues in the Department of Philosophy at the University of Vermont, and I am grateful for their original collaboration.

We reason every day of our lives. Whether the topic is politics, morality, movies, or sports, we offer arguments to convince others that our views are reasonable. But what is an argument, and which arguments should be accepted?

Arguments

In ordinary parlance, an argument is simply a dispute. To philosophers, however, an argument is a collection of sentences consisting of one or more *premises* and a *conclusion*. The evidence you cite is your premise or premises; the statement you defend is your conclusion. Whenever you construct an argument, you need to take some claim as your premise. Of course, assuming the truth of a controversial claim in order to argue for what is obvious would be unconvincing. The direction of sensible argumentation is always from the more obvious to the less. Ideally, a reasoner will choose premises that are uncontroversial and argue that a more disputed, perhaps even surprising, conclusion follows from those unproblematic assumptions.

Logic is the branch of philosophy that studies the relations between premises and conclusion, establishing guidelines about which claims can be inferred from others. This task has been carried out with great success for deductive inference.

Deductive Arguments

The central concept of deductive logic is *validity*. An argument is valid whenever the truth of the premises guarantees the truth of the conclusion. In other words, in a valid argument the conclusion follows from the premises; that is, the conclusion cannot be false if the premises are true. Logic is not concerned with the truth of the premises or the truth of the conclusion but only with the relation between the premises and the conclusion.

In ordinary English "valid" and "true" are often used synonymously, yet their technical meanings are different. In philosophical terminology, statements are true or false, not valid or invalid. Arguments, however, are valid or invalid, not true or false. Thus you can make a true statement or present a valid argument, but you can't speak validly or argue truthfully.

Note that a valid argument can have true or false premises, and they may be as numerous as wished. Here, for example, is a valid argument with true premises (such an argument is referred to as a *sound argument*):

PREMISE 1 The capital of Massachusetts is Boston.
PREMISE 2 Boston is the home of the Boston Red Sox.
CONCLUSION The capital of Massachusetts is the home of the Boston Red Sox.

In this example the two premises are true, and the conclusion follows from the premises.

Here is another valid argument, but in this case the first premise is false and the second is true.

PREMISE 1	All playwrights lived in Greece.
PREMISE 2	Shakespeare was a playwright.
CONCLUSION	Shakespeare lived in Greece.

Although the first premise is false, the argument is nevertheless valid, because the conclusion follows from the premises. In other words, whether the premises are true, they imply the conclusion.

Now here is another valid argument, but this time both premises are false, yet they imply a true conclusion:

PREMISE 1	All canaries are polar bears.
PREMISE 2	All polar bears have feathers.
CONCLUSION	All canaries have feathers.

Note also that even if the premises of an argument are all true and the conclusion is true, the argument may not be valid, as in this case:

PREMISE 1	Some roses are red.
PREMISE 2	Some violets are blue.
CONCLUSION	Flowers give some people hay fever.

The problem is that while all the statements are true, the truth of the premises does not guarantee the truth of the conclusion, and that relation is the hallmark of a valid argument.

Thus a compelling deductive argument should be valid. Otherwise the premises will not lead us to accept the conclusion.

Deductive arguments, however, are not the only form of effective reasoning. We turn next to non-deductive arguments.

Non-Deductive Arguments

We encounter many good but non-deductive inferences in everyday and scientific discussions. Suppose, for example, that a particular drug is given a hundred thousand trials across a wide variety of people, and it never produces serious side effects. Even the most scrupulous researcher would conclude that the drug is safe. Still, this conclusion cannot be deductively inferred from the data. Here is the argument:

PREMISE	In 100,000 trials, drug X produced no serious side effects.
CONCLUSION	Drug X does not have any serious side effects.

Because a serious side effect may appear on the 100,001st trial, the premise could be true even though the conclusion is false. Hence the argument is deductively invalid, yet it is strong and should be accepted.

We can present many more good but deductively invalid arguments. Here is another example.

PREMISE 1	The dining room window is shattered.
PREMISE 2	A baseball is lying in the middle of the glass on the dining room floor.
PREMISE 3	A baseball bat is found on the ground in the yard outside the dining room.
CONCLUSION	The dining room window was shattered by being hit with a baseball.

If we recognize only the standard of deductive validity, then the previous arguments—and all other arguments like these—will have to be dismissed as bad reasoning. That constraint on argumentation, however, is unacceptable. Why should we demand that the truth of the premises guarantees the truth of the conclusion? After all, we often suppose that a claim is not certain but highly probable. For instance, we would be willing to place a sizable bet that a roulette ball will not land on number 7 twenty times in a row. Yet no true premises about how roulette is played render that result impossible. Logic, therefore, has a second task. It needs to provide criteria for evaluating good but non-deductive inferences.

Induction

We believe that if a dry piece of paper is placed into the flame of a candle, the paper will burn. Why do we hold this belief? We reason that in the past dry paper placed into the flame of a candle always burned, so we infer that it will burn in the present case. This common type of reasoning is called *induction*. In it, we rely on similar, observed cases to infer that the same event or property will recur in as yet unobserved cases.

Of course, in different instances we have different amounts of evidence on which to draw. If only ten cases of a disease have been observed, then we will have much less confidence in predicting the course of the disease than if we had observed ten thousand cases. Philosophers often refer to our confidence in a claim as our *strength of belief*. Surely it should increase with the number of positive instances of the claim. Hence, for example, if you arrive in a new town and notice that all the buses you see on your first day are green, then as the days pass and you continue to observe only green buses, the strength of your belief that all the buses in town are green will increase.

While positive instances gradually confirm an inductive generalization, rendering it more and more reasonable, a negative instance defeats the generalization. To take a dramatic twentieth-century example, with the splitting of the first atom, the long-standing claim that atoms are indivisible particles of matter had to be relinquished.

Beside the sheer number of positive instances, another criterion for good inductive reasoning is that the evidence be varied. If you have observed buses in many different parts of town, then you are more justified in claiming that the town's buses are all green than if you have only considered the buses on your own street.

Hypothesis Testing

All of us, especially scientists, test hypotheses as a form of non-deductive reasoning. For example, imagine that a problem has developed in a small rural town, where residents are falling sick at an alarming rate. The local doctor hypothesizes that the trouble has been caused by the opening of a new chemical plant that is emptying waste within a mile of one of the lakes that yields the town's supply of drinking water. The hypothesis can be tested in a number of different ways. For instance, the residents might check the consequences of drinking water only from a lake not close to the chemical plant. Granted, the doctor's hypothesis would fail such a test if, despite using water from a different lake, the sickness continued to spread. Yet the hypothesis might pass the test if drinking water from a different lake leads to the illness disappearing. This case indicates the way in which a hypothesis can be tested. Frequently we advance a claim whose truth or falsity we are unable to ascertain by direct observation. We cannot just look and see if the earth moves, or if the continents were once part of a single land mass, or if the butler committed the crime. In evaluating such hypotheses, we consider what things we would expect to observe if the hypothesis were true. Then we investigate to see if these expectations are confirmed. If so, then the hypothesis passes the test, and its success counts in its favor; if not, then the failure counts against the hypothesis.

Inference to the Best Explanation

Another common and indispensable type of non-deductible inference should be familiar to readers of detective stories. Sherlock Holmes, for instance, uses this type of reasoning in his first encounter with Dr. Watson in *A Study in Scarlet*.

> I *knew* you came from Afghanistan. From long habit the train of thoughts ran so swiftly through my mind that I arrived at the conclusion without being conscious of intermediate steps. There were such steps, however. The train of reasoning ran, 'Here is a gentleman of a medical type, but with the air of a military man. Clearly an army doctor, then. He has just come from the tropics, for his face is dark, and that is not the natural tint of his skin, for his wrists are fair. He has undergone hardship and sickness, as his haggard face says clearly. His left arm has been injured. He holds it in a stiff and unnatural manner. Where in the tropics could an English army doctor have seen much hardship and got his arm wounded? Clearly in Afghanistan.' The whole train of thought did not occupy a second. I then remarked that you came from Afghanistan, and you were astonished.[1]

Holmes's argument is deductively invalid. Even though Watson has a deep tan and a wounded arm, perhaps he has never been in Afghanistan but obtained the tan in Argentina and the wound in a knife fight in Peru. Yet Holmes's argument does provide considerable support for his claim that Watson had been in Afghanistan. Here is how Holmes's reasoning works. He lists various facts, such as the military bearing, the tan, and the wounded arm. Then he uses them to infer a conclusion that would explain all of them. In this case, if Watson is a military doctor who just returned from active service in Afghanistan, that conclusion would explain why he has a tan, an injured arm, and so forth. The name for this type of reasoning is *argument by inference to the best explanation*, and it is closely related to hypothesis testing. There a hypothesis is supported when observations that can be deduced from the hypothesis are borne out. In argument by inference to the best explanation, the hypothesis is supported when it explains given facts. In either case the results can yield high probabilities, although not certainties.

Argument Analysis

Having examined various types of inference, let us now consider how this information may be used in analyzing reasoning. The basic task of argument analysis is to provide a clear formulation of the chain of argumentation presented in a piece of prose. After all, arguments do not come neatly packaged with labels clearly identifying the premises and the conclusion. A critic needs to find the optimal version of an argument before evaluating it. Perhaps surprisingly, the first step to assess reasoning is finding the conclusion. It may occur at the beginning, at the end, or in the middle of a passage. Indeed, the conclusion may not be stated at all. Thus to find it, you need to ask: "What is the author trying to persuade us to believe?"

After locating the conclusion, the next step is to list the premises. To find them, you need to consider the author's starting places. Once they are found, you are ready to try to trace a plausible route from the premises to the conclusion. Here you need to clarify the meanings of key terms and consider the criteria for different types of inference. Once you have reconstructed the argument, you can appraise its success or failure.

Evaluating reasoning is a complex task, because human language is rich and fluid, and facts can be connected in many ways. Yet while the task is difficult, the alternative is unacceptable. For if we give up trying to understand reasoning, then we must either naively accept what others assert or abandon the possibility of assessing their claims.

Note

1 *A Study in Scarlet*, in Sir Arthur Conan Doyle, *The Complete Sherlock Holmes* (Garden City, NY: Doubleday, n.d.), 24.

2
Necessary and Sufficient Conditions

Fallacies are mistakes in reasoning, and they may be found in many varieties. One committed surprisingly frequently, even in sophisticated conversations, involves a confusion of two crucial concepts. The first is known as a "necessary condition," the second as a "sufficient condition." What these terms mean and how they relate to each other is our next topic.

One state of affairs, A, is a necessary condition for another state of affairs, B, if B cannot occur without A occurring. For instance, in the United States a person must be at least eighteen years old before being entitled to vote. In other words, being eighteen is a necessary condition for being entitled to vote.

One state of affairs, A, is a sufficient condition for another state of affairs, B, if the occurrence of A ensures the occurrence of B. For instance, in an American presidential election for a candidate to receive 300 electoral votes ensures that candidate's election. In other words, receiving 300 electoral votes is a sufficient condition for winning the election.

Note that even if A is a necessary condition for B, A need not be a sufficient condition for B. For instance, even if you need to be eighteen to vote, you also need to be a citizen of the United States. Thus being eighteen is necessary but not sufficient for voting.

Similarly, even if A is a sufficient condition for B, A need not be a necessary condition for B. For instance, if a presidential candidate receives 300 electoral votes, then that candidate is elected, but receiving 300 electoral votes, while sufficient for election, is not necessary, because a candidate who receives 299 votes is also elected.

Confusing necessary and sufficient conditions is a common mistake in reasoning. If one individual argues that extensive prior experience in Washington, DC is required for a person to be a worthy presidential candidate, that claim is not refuted by pointing out that many candidates with such experience have not been worthy. To refute the claim that experience is necessary for worthiness requires demonstrating not that many with experience have been unworthy but that a person without experience *has* been worthy. After all, the original claim was that experience is necessary, not sufficient.

Suppose A is both necessary and sufficient for B. For example, being a rectangle with all four sides equal is necessary and sufficient for being a square. In other words, a geometric figure cannot be a square unless it is a rectangle with all four sides equal, and if a rectangle has all four sides equal, then it is a square. Thus a satisfactory definition of "square" is "rectangle with all four sides equal."

Now here is an additional twist that may be surprising. What is the difference between asserting that A is a necessary condition for B and that B is a sufficient condition for A? Nothing. These are two ways of saying that the occurrence of B ensures the occurrence of A. Furthermore, what is the difference between asserting that A is a sufficient condition for B and that B is a necessary condition for A? Again, nothing. These are two ways of saying that the occurrence of A ensures the occurrence of B.

The critical mistake is thinking that if A is necessary for B, then A is sufficient for B. Or that if A is sufficient for B, then A is necessary for B. These are fallacies.

Hence the next time you hear someone say, for example, that you can be well educated without knowing any logic, because some people who know logic are not well educated, you can point out that the speaker has confused necessary and sufficient conditions. Just because some people who know logic are not well educated does not prove that you can be well educated without knowing logic. That conclusion would follow only if some people who don't know logic are nevertheless well educated.

If you are on the lookout for this fallacy, you will find it committed far more often than you might suppose.

3
Dummy Hypotheses

Why is reason preferable to alternative methods for deciding what to believe? The answer lies not in the infallibility of reason but in its capacity for self-correction. Only if our theories may be shown to be wrong are they useful in guiding action.

To hold to an explanation of events in the face of conflicting facts is not to protect one's view but to render it pointless. As an illustration of this principle, consider the following anecdote, found in Anita Shreve's novel *All He Ever Wanted*:

> A man is propelled one minute sooner to his automobile because he decides not to stop to kiss his wife good-bye. As a consequence of this omission, he then crosses a bridge one minute before it collapses, taking all its traffic and doomed souls into the swirling and angry depths below. Oblivious, and safely out of harm's way, our man continues on his journey.[1]

Let us first suppose this man believes that he is protected by angels who watch over him to ensure his safety. What are we to make of this claim?

To begin with, the angels' concern did not extend to the many others who fell to their death. How is their tragedy to be explained? Our man does not know, but when he ponders the matter, he is likely to suppose that the chain of events serves a purpose that lies beyond human understanding.

Next, suppose this man does not believe in angels but in demons, to whom he attributes this disaster. What are we to make of this claim? Note that any evil the demons displayed in these horrific events did not extend to the man himself, for he was saved. How is the malevolence of the demons compatible with this man's good fortune? He does not know, but when he ponders the matter, he is likely to suppose that the chain of events serves a purpose that lies beyond human understanding.

A third hypothesis the man might accept is that the world is the scene of a struggle between angels and demons. Assume both have some but not all power. When events go well, the angels' benevolence is in the ascendancy; when events go badly, the demons' malevolence is in the ascendancy. In the tragic case under consideration the demons caused the collapse of the bridge, while the angels arranged for the one man to be saved.

Is this third explanation unnecessarily complex and therefore to be rejected? No, for even though in one sense it is more complex than the other two, because it involves two sorts of supernatural beings rather than only one, in another sense the third explanation is simpler than the other two, because it leaves no aspect of the situation beyond human understanding.

The crucial point is that all three hypotheses (as well as innumerable others of this sort that one might imagine) can be maintained regardless of the facts. For instance, suppose the bridge had collapsed at a time when all vehicles but one had already crossed. Then a person who believes in angels would thank them for having saved the lives of so many, while considering mysterious why the one vehicle was lost; the person who believes in demons would attribute the loss of the one vehicle to their work, while considering mysterious why the lives of so many were saved; the person who believes in angels and demons would thank the angels for having saved the lives of so many, while attributing the loss of the one vehicle to the work of the demons.

Any of these incompatible hypotheses can be interpreted to account for whatever events occur. Using them in this way turns them into dummy hypotheses, compatible with all possible facts.

Like a dummy bell rope that makes no sound, a dummy hypothesis makes no sense. Its compatibility with all possible situations robs it of any explanatory power.

Contrast a dummy hypothesis with a scientific one, which, to reiterate, is typically tested by the following four-step procedure:

1) Formulate the hypothesis clearly;
2) Work out the implications of the hypothesis;
3) Perform experiments to verify whether these implications hold;
4) Observe the consequences of these experiments and, as a result, accept or reject the hypothesis.

In practice, complications may abound at each stage. Moreover, as we noted previously, this inductive method yields only high probabilities, not certainties, for a hypothesis may pass numerous tests, yet fail additional ones. The crucial point, though, is that scientific hypotheses are tested, then rejected if inconsistent with the outcome of the tests.

As an example of how scientific method works, consider the case of the American army surgeon Dr. Walter Reed (1851–1902), who sought to control yellow fever. He hypothesized that the disease was caused by a specific type of mosquito. To test this hypothesis, he quarantined some individuals so that they would not come into contact with any of the insects, but did not quarantine the other test subjects. When those exposed developed the disease and those quarantined did not, Reed had strong evidence that the mosquitoes were the cause of the disease.

Had the results of the experiment been different, Reed's hypothesis might have turned out to be false. If those quarantined had developed the disease at the same rate as those exposed, then Reed would have rejected his hypothesis and been led to develop and test others.

That a hypothesis can be disproved by testing is not a weakness of the hypothesis but a strength. Any genuine hypothesis is open to possible refutation. Dummy hypotheses are not and thus do not provide understanding. They may be psychologically comforting but do not enable us to gain control over our environment.

Some may choose to attribute an outbreak of yellow fever to angels or demons or a struggle between them. Such hypotheses are untestable, however, and therefore do not help eradicate or control the disease.

Finally, a few thoughts about the story of the fallen bridge with which we began. Why did it collapse? The answer is most likely to be found by calling in engineers who can determine the cause, learn from the case, and build a new bridge that will be safer. At no point, however, will they rely on theories involving angelic or demonic beings.

Yet some may persist in asking why the one man was saved. The answer is that he arrived one minute sooner because of not stopping to kiss his wife goodbye. Why didn't he kiss his wife goodbye? Perhaps he was distracted by thoughts of an upcoming business meeting. Why was that meeting so critical? We can continue such speculation endlessly, but the key point is that no question we may raise will be answered satisfactorily by appealing to any dummy hypothesis.

Note

1 Anita Shreve, *All He Ever Wanted* (Boston: Little Brown and Company, 2005), 79.

PART II: FREE WILL

4
Determinism and Freedom

We turn now to one of the most discussed philosophical questions: Do human beings ever act freely? You may assume they do. Consider an ordinary human action, for instance, waving to a friend. You believe you have the power to do so and the power not to. The choice is yours.

Equally obvious, however, is that whenever an event occurs, a causal explanation can account for the occurrence of the event. If you feel a pain in your arm, then something is causing that pain. If nothing were causing it, you wouldn't be in pain. The same line of reasoning applies whether the event to be explained is a loud noise, a change in the weather, or an individual's action. If the event were uncaused, it wouldn't have occurred. Yet if all actions are part of a causal claim extending back beyond your birth, how can any of your actions be free?

Our discussion of these conflicting considerations begins with an account of one of the twentieth century's most famous criminal trials. How did it involve the issue of determinism and freedom? Let us see.

In 1924 the American people were horrified by a senseless crime of extraordinary brutality. The defendants were eighteen-year-old Nathan Leopold and seventeen-year-old Richard Loeb, the sons of Chicago millionaires, and brilliant students who had led seemingly idyllic lives. Leopold was the youngest graduate in the history of the University of Chicago, and Loeb the youngest graduate in the history of the University of Michigan. Suddenly they were accused of the kidnapping and vicious murder of fourteen-year-old Bobby

Franks, a cousin of Loeb's. Before the trial even began, Leopold and Loeb both confessed, and from across the country came an outcry for their execution.

The lawyer who agreed to defend them was Clarence Darrow, the outstanding defense attorney of his time. Because Leopold and Loeb had already admitted their crime, Darrow's only chance was to explain their behavior in such a way that his clients could escape the death penalty. He was forced to argue that Leopold and Loeb were not morally responsible for what they had done, that they were not to be blamed for their actions. But how could he possibly maintain that position?

Darrow's defense was a landmark in the history of criminal law. He argued that the actions of his clients resulted from hereditary and environmental forces beyond their control.[1] Leopold suffered from a glandular disease that left him depressed and moody. Originally shy with girls, he had been sent to an all-girls school as a cure but had sustained deep psychic scars from which he never recovered. In addition, his parents instilled in him the belief that his wealth absolved him of any responsibility toward others. Pathologically inferior because of his diminutive size, and pathologically superior because of his wealth, he became an acute schizophrenic.

Loeb suffered from a nervous disorder that caused fainting spells. During his unhappy childhood, he had often thought of committing suicide. He was under the control of a domineering governess and was forced to lie and cheat to deceive her. His wealth led him to believe that he was superior to all those around him, and he developed a fascination for crime, an activity in which he could demonstrate his superiority. By the time he reached college he was severely psychotic.

In his final plea Darrow recounted these facts. His central theme was that Leopold and Loeb were in the grip of powers beyond their control, that they themselves were victims.

> I do not know what it was that made these boys do this mad act, but I do know there is a reason for it. I know they did not

> beget themselves. I know that any one of an infinite number of causes reaching back to the beginning might be working out in these boys' minds, whom you are asked to hang in malice and in hatred and in injustice, because someone in the past has sinned against them ... What had this boy to do with it? He was not his own father; he was not his own mother; he was not his own grandparents. All of this was handed to him. He did not surround himself with governesses and wealth. He did not make himself. And yet he is to be compelled to pay.[2]

Darrow's plea was successful, for Leopold and Loeb escaped execution and were sentenced to life imprisonment. Although they had committed crimes and were legally responsible for their actions, the judge believed they were not morally responsible, for they had not acted freely.

If the line of argument that Darrow utilized in the Leopold-Loeb case is sound, then not only were Leopold and Loeb not to blame for what they had done, but no person is ever to blame for any actions. As Darrow himself put it, "We are all helpless."[3] But is Darrow's argument sound? Does the conclusion follow from the premises, and are the premises true?

We can formalize his argument as follows:

PREMISE 1 No action is free if it must occur.

PREMISE 2 In the case of every event that occurs, prior conditions, known or unknown, ensure the event's occurrence.

CONCLUSION Therefore no action is free.

Premise (1) assumes that an action is free only if it is within the agent's power to perform it and within the agent's power not to perform it. In other words, whether a free action will occur is up to the agent. If circumstances require the agent to perform a certain action or require the agent not to perform it, then the action is not free.

Premise (2) is the thesis known as *determinism*. Put graphically, it is the claim that if at any time a being knew the position of every particle in the universe and all the forces acting on each particle, then that being could predict with certainty every future event. Determinism does not presume such a being exists; the being is only imagined in order to illustrate what the world would be like if determinism were true.

Darrow's conclusion, which is supposed to follow from premises (1) and (2), is that no person has free will. Note that to have free will does not imply being free with regard to all actions, for only the mythical Superman is free to leap tall buildings at a single bound. But so long as at least some of an agent's actions are free, the agent is said to have free will. What Darrow's argument purports to prove is that not a single human action that has ever been performed has been performed freely.

Does the conclusion of Darrow's argument follow from the premises? If premise (2) is true, then every event that occurs must occur, for its occurrence is ensured by antecedent conditions. Because every action is an event, it follows from premise (2) that every action that occurs must occur. But according to premise (1), no action is free if it must occur. Thus if premises (1) and (2) are true, it follows that no action is free—the conclusion of Darrow's argument.

Even granting that Darrow's reasoning is valid, we need not accept the conclusion of his argument unless we grant the truth of his premises. Should we do so?

Hard determinism is the view that both premises of Darrow's argument are correct. In other words, a hard determinist believes that determinism is true and that, as a consequence, no person has free will.[4] Determinists note that whenever an event occurs, we all assume that a causal explanation can account for the occurrence of the event. Suppose, for example, you feel a pain in your arm and are prompted to visit a physician. After examining you, the doctor announces that the pain has no cause, either physical or psychological.

In other words, you are supposed to be suffering from an uncaused pain. On hearing this diagnosis, you would surely switch doctors. After all, no one may be able to discover the cause of your pain, but surely something is causing it. If nothing were causing it, you wouldn't be in pain. This same line of reasoning applies whether the event to be explained is a loud noise, a change in the weather, or an individual's action. If the event were uncaused, it wouldn't have occurred.

We may agree, however, that the principle of determinism holds in the vast majority of cases, yet doubt its applicability in the realm of human action. While causal explanations may be found for rocks falling and birds flying, people are more complex than rocks or birds.

The determinist responds to this objection by asking us to consider any specific action: for instance, your decision to read this book. You may suppose your decision was uncaused, but did you not wish to acquire information about philosophy? The determinist argues that your desire for such information, together with your belief that the information is found in this book, caused you to read. Just as physical forces cause rocks and birds to do things, so human actions are caused by desires and beliefs.

If you doubt this claim, the determinist can call attention to our success in predicting people's behavior. For example, a store owner who reduces prices can depend on increasing visits by shoppers; an athlete who wins a major championship can rely on greater attention from the press. Furthermore, when we read novels or see plays, we expect to understand why the characters act as they do, and an author who fails to provide such explanations is charged with poor writing. The similarity of people's reactions to the human condition also accounts for the popularity of the incisive psychological insights of a writer such as the French aphorist La Rochefoucauld (1613–80). We read one of his maxims, for instance, "When our integrity declines, our taste does also,"[5] and nod our heads with approval, but are we not agreeing to a plausible generalization about the workings of the human psyche?

Granted, people's behavior cannot be predicted with certainty, but the hard determinist reminds us that each individual is influenced by a unique combination of hereditary and environmental factors. Just as each rock is slightly different from every other rock, and each bird is somewhat different from every other bird, so human beings differ from each other. Yet just as rocks and birds are part of an unbroken chain of causes and effects, so human beings, too, are part of that chain. Just as a rock falls because it breaks off from a cliff, so people act because of their desires and beliefs. And just as a rock has no control over the wind that causes it to break off, so people have no control over the desires and beliefs that cause them to act. In short, we are said to have no more control over our desires and beliefs than Leopold and Loeb had over theirs. If you can control your desire for food and your friend cannot, the explanation is that your will is of a sort that can control your desire, and your friend's will is of a sort that cannot. That your will is of one sort and your friend's will of another is not within the control of either of you. As hard determinist John Hospers (1918–2011) wrote, "If we can overcome the effects of early environment, the ability to do so is itself a product of the early environment. We did not give ourselves this ability; and if we lack it we cannot be blamed for not having it."[6]

At this point in the argument an anti-determinist is apt to call attention to recent developments in physics that have been interpreted by some thinkers as a refutation of determinism. They claim that work in quantum mechanics demonstrates that certain subatomic events are uncaused and inherently unpredictable. Yet some physicists and philosophers of science argue that determinism has not been refuted, because the experimental results can be understood in causal terms.[7] The outcome of this dispute, however, seems irrelevant to the issue of human freedom, because the events we are discussing are not subatomic, and indeterminism on that level may be compatible with the universal causation of events on the much larger level of human action.

Here, then, is a summary of hard determinism. According to this view, determinism is true and no person has free will. Every event that occurs is caused to occur, for otherwise why would it occur? Your present actions are events caused by your previous desires and beliefs, which themselves are accounted for by hereditary and environmental factors. These are part of a causal chain extending back far beyond your birth, and each link of the chain determines the succeeding link. Because you obviously have no control over events that occurred before your birth, and because these earlier events determined the latter ones, what follows is that you have no control over your present actions. In sum, you do not have free will.

The hard determinist's argument may appear plausible, yet few are inclined to accept its shocking conclusion. They opt, therefore, to deny one of its two premises. *Soft determinism* is the view that the conclusion is false because premise (1) is false. In other words, a soft determinist believes both that determinism is true and that human beings have free will. The implication of the position is that an action may be free even if it is part of a causal chain extending back to events outside the agent's control. While at first this view may appear implausible, it has been defended throughout the centuries by many eminent philosophers, including David Hume (1711–76) and John Stuart Mill (1806–73).

An approach employed explicitly or implicitly by many soft determinists has come to be known as *the paradigm-case argument*. Consider it first in another setting, where its use is a classic of philosophical argumentation.

In studying physics, we learn that ordinary objects like tables and chairs are composed of sparsely scattered, minute particles. This finding may lead us to suppose that such objects are not solid. As physicist Sir Arthur Eddington (1882–1944) put it, a "plank has no solidity of substance. To step on it is like stepping on a swarm of flies."[8]

Eddington's view that a plank is not solid was forcefully attacked by philosopher L. Susan Stebbing (1885–1943). She pointed out that the word *solid* derives its meaning from examples such as planks.

> For "solid" just is the word we use to describe a certain respect in which a plank of wood resembles a block of marble, a piece of paper, and a cricket ball, and in which each of these differs from a sponge, from the interior of a soap-bubble, and from the holes in a net.... The point is that the common usage of language enables us to attribute a meaning to the phrase *a solid plank*; but there is no common usage of language that provides a meaning for the word *solid* that would make sense to say that the plank on which I stand is not solid.[9]

In other words, a plank is a paradigm (or standard) case of solidity. Anyone who claims that a plank is not solid does not know how the word *solid* is used in the English language. Note that Stebbing was not criticizing Eddington's scientific views but only the manner in which he interpreted them.

The paradigm-case argument is useful to soft determinists, for in the face of the hard determinist's claim that no human action is free, soft determinists respond by pointing to a paradigm case of a free action, for instance, a person walking down the street. They stipulate that the individual is not under the influence of drugs, is not attached to ropes, is not sleepwalking, and so on; in brief, they refer to a normal, everyday instance of a person walking down the street. Soft determinists claim that the behavior described is a paradigm case of a free action, clearly distinguishable from instances in which a person is, in fact, under the influence of drugs, attached to ropes, or sleepwalking. These latter cases are not examples of free actions, or are at best problematic examples, while the case the soft determinists cite is clear and seemingly indisputable. Indeed, according to soft determinists, anyone who claims that the act of walking down the street is not free does not know how the word *free* is used in English. Thus people certainly have free will, for we can cite obvious cases in which they act freely.

How do soft determinists define a *free action*? According to them, actions are free if the persons who perform them wish to do so and could, if they wished, not perform them. If your arm is forcibly raised, you did not act freely, for you did not wish to raise your arm. If you were locked in a room, you would also not be free, even if you wished to be there, for if you wished to leave, you couldn't.

Soft determinists emphasize that once we define *freedom* correctly, any apparent incompatibility between freedom and determinism disappears. Consider some particular action I perform that is free in the sense explicated by soft determinists. Even if the action is one link in a causal chain extending far back beyond my birth, nevertheless I am free with regard to that action, for I wish to perform it, and if I did not wish to, I would not do so. This description of the situation is consistent with supposing that my wish is a result of hereditary and environmental factors over which I have no control. The presence of such factors is, according to the soft determinists, irrelevant to the question of whether my action is free. I may be walking down a particular street because of my desire to buy a coat and my belief that I am heading toward a clothing store, and this desire and belief may themselves be caused by any number of other factors. But because I desire to walk down the street and could walk down some other street if I so desired, it follows that I am freely walking down the street. By this line of reasoning soft determinists affirm both free will and determinism, finding no incompatibility between them.

Soft determinism is an inviting doctrine, for it allows us to maintain a belief in free will without having to relinquish the belief that every event has a cause. Soft determinism, however, is open to objections that have led some philosophers to reject the position.

As they see it, the fundamental problem for soft determinists is that their definition of *freedom* is not in accord with the ordinary way in which we use the term. Note that soft determinists and hard determinists offer two different definitions of *freedom*. According to the hard determinist, an action is free if it is within my power to perform it and also within my power not to perform it. According to the soft determinist, an action is free if it is such that if I wish to perform it I can, and if I wish not to perform it I also can. To highlight the difference between these definitions, consider the case of a man who has been hypnotized and rolls up the leg of his pants as if to cross a stream. Is his action free? According to the hard determinist, the man's action is not free, for it is not within his power to refrain from rolling up the leg of his pants. According to the soft determinist's definition of *freedom*, the action seems to be free, for the agent desires to perform it, and if he didn't desire to, he wouldn't. But a man under hypnosis is not free. Therefore the soft determinist's definition of *freedom* strikes some as unsatisfactory.

Perhaps this objection to soft determinism is unfair, because the desires of the hypnotized man are not his own but are controlled by the hypnotist. The force of the objection to soft determinism, however, is that the soft determinist does not focus on whether a person's wishes or desires are themselves within that individual's control. The hard determinist emphasizes that my action is free only if it is up to me whether to perform it. But in order for an action to be up to me, don't I need to have control over my own wishes or desires? If not, my desires might be controlled by a hypnotist, a brainwasher, my family, hereditary factors, and so on, and thus I would not be free. According to soft determinists, however, I would be free even if my desires were not within my control, so long as I was acting according to my desires and could act differently if my desires were different. But could my desires have been different? If not, then I could not have acted in any way other than I did, which is the description of a person who is not free. Thus runs the argument against soft determinism.

What of the soft determinist's claim that a person's walking down the street is a paradigm case of a free action? Although many would agree that the paradigm-case argument can sometimes be used effectively, the soft determinist's appeal to it may not be convincing. To see why, imagine that we traveled to a land in which the inhabitants believed that every woman born on February 29 was a witch, and that every witch had the power to cause droughts. If we refused to believe that any woman was a witch, the philosophically sophisticated inhabitants might try to convince us by appealing to the paradigm-case argument, claiming that any woman born on February 29 is a paradigm case of a witch.

What would we say in response? How does this appeal to a paradigm case differ from Stebbing's appeal to a plank as a paradigm case of solidity? No one doubts that a plank can hold significant weight and is, in that sense, solid. But until women born on February 29 demonstrate the power to cause droughts and are, in that sense, witches, the mere linguistic claim that any woman born on February 29 is a witch is in danger of having no force.

Are soft determinists appealing to an indisputable instance when they claim that a person's walking down the street is a paradigm case of a free action? Perhaps not, for as we saw in the trial of Leopold and Loeb, such apparently free actions may not turn out to be judged as free. Critics argue that by appealing to a disputable example as a paradigm case, soft determinists assume what they are supposed to be proving, an error known as *begging the question*. They are supposed to demonstrate that actions such as walking down the street are examples of free actions. Merely asserting that such actions are free is to overlook the hard determinist's argument that such actions are not free. No questionable instances can be used as a paradigm case, and walking down the street appears to be, as Darrow demonstrated, a questionable example of a free action. Thus soft determinism appears to some philosophers to have a serious weakness.

Remember that the hard determinist argues that because premises (1) and (2) of Darrow's argument are true, so is the conclusion. Soft determinists argue that premise (1) is false. If they are mistaken (and many philosophers believe they are not), then the only way to avoid hard determinism is to reject premise (2). That position is known as *libertarianism.* The libertarian agrees with the hard determinist that if an action must occur, then it is not free. For the libertarian as well as for the hard determinist, I am free with regard to a particular action only if it is within my power to perform the action and within my power not to perform it.

But do persons ever act freely? The hard determinist believes that people are never free, because in the case of every action, antecedent conditions, known or unknown, ensure the action's occurrence. Libertarians refuse to accept this conclusion but find it impossible to reject premise (1) of Darrow's argument. Therefore their only recourse is to reject premise (2). As Sherlock Holmes noted, "When you have eliminated the impossible, whatever remains, however improbable, must be the truth."[10] The libertarian thus denies that every event has a cause.

Why is the libertarian so convinced that people sometimes act freely? Consider an ordinary human action, for instance, raising your hand at a meeting to attract the speaker's attention. If you are attending a lecture and time comes for questions from the audience, you believe it within your power to raise your hand and also within your power not to. The choice is yours. Nothing forces you to ask a question, and nothing prevents you from asking one. What could be more obvious? If this description of the situation is accurate, then hard determinism is incorrect, for you are free with regard to the act of raising your hand.

The heart of the libertarian's position is that innumerable examples of this sort are conclusive evidence for free will. Indeed, we normally accept them as such. We assume on most occasions that we are free with regard to our actions, and, moreover, we assume that other persons are free with regard to theirs. If a friend agrees to meet us at six o'clock for dinner and arrives an hour late claiming to have lost track of time, we blame him for his tardiness, because we assume he had it within his power to act otherwise. All he had to do was glance at his watch, and assuming no special circumstances were involved, it was within his power to do so. He was simply negligent and deserves to be blamed, for he could have acted conscientiously. But to believe he could have acted in a way other than he did is to believe he was free.

How do hard determinists respond to such examples? They argue that such situations need to be examined in greater detail. In the case of our friend who arrives an hour late for dinner, we assume he is to blame for his actions, but the hard determinist points out that some motive impelled him to be late. Perhaps he was more interested in finishing his work at the office than in arriving on time for dinner. But why was he more interested in finishing his work than in arriving on time? Perhaps his parents had instilled in him the importance of work but not promptness. Hard determinists stress that whatever the explanation for his lateness, the motive causing it was stronger than the motive impelling him to arrive on time. He acted as he did because his strongest motive prevailed. Which motive was the strongest, however, was not within his control, and thus he was not free.

The hard determinist's reply may seem persuasive. How can I deny that I am invariably caused to act by my strongest motive? Analysis suggests, however, that the thesis may be what I earlier termed a "dummy hypothesis," immune from refutation, and so devoid of empirical content. No matter what example of a human action is presented, a defender of the thesis could argue that the person's action resulted from the strongest motive. If I take a swim, taking a swim was my strongest motive. If I decide to forgo the swim and read a book instead, then reading a book was my strongest motive. How do we know that my motive to read a book was stronger than my motive to take a swim? Because I read a book and did not take a swim. If this line of argument appears powerful, the illusion will last only so long as we do not ask how we are to identify a person's strongest motive. The only possible answer appears to be that the strongest motive is the motive that prevails, the motive that causes the person to act. If the strongest motive is the motive causing the person to act, what force is in the claim that the motive causing a person to act is causing the person to act? No insight into the complexities of human action is obtained by trumpeting such a redundancy.

Thus the hard determinist does not so easily succeed in overturning the examples of free actions offered by the libertarian. However, both hard and soft determinists have another argument to offer against the libertarian's position. If the libertarian is correct that free actions are uncaused, why do they occur? Are they inexplicable occurrences? If so, to act freely would be to act in a random, chaotic, unintelligible fashion. Yet holding people morally blameworthy for inexplicable actions strikes most as unreasonable. If you are driving a car and, to your surprise, find yourself turning the wheel to the right, we can hardly blame you if an accident occurs, for what happened was beyond your control.

Hence determinists argue that libertarians are caught in a dilemma. If we are caused to do whatever we do, libertarians assert we are not morally responsible for our actions. Yet if our actions are uncaused and inexplicable, libertarians again must deny our moral responsibility. How then can libertarians claim we ever act responsibly?

To understand the libertarian response, consider the simple act of a woman picking up a cell phone. Suppose we want to understand what she is doing and are told she is calling her stockbroker. The woman has decided to buy some stock and wishes her broker to place the appropriate order. With this explanation, we now know why this woman has picked up the phone. Although we may be interested in learning more about the woman or her choice of stocks, we have a complete explanation of her action, which turns out not to be random, chaotic, or unintelligible. We may not know what, if anything, is causing the woman to act, but we do know the reason for her action. The libertarian thus replies to the determinist's dilemma by arguing that an action can be uncaused yet understandable, explicable in terms of the agent's intentions or purposes.

Now contrast the libertarian's description of a particular action with a determinist's. Let the action be your moving your arm to adjust your radio. A determinist claims you were caused to move your arm by your desire to adjust the radio and your belief that you could make this adjustment by turning the dials. A libertarian claims you moved your arm in order to adjust the set.

Note that the libertarian explains human actions fundamentally differently from the way in which we explain the movement of rocks or rivers. If we speak of a rock's purpose in falling off a cliff or a river's purpose in flowing south, we do so only metaphorically, for we believe that rocks and rivers have no purposes of their own but are caused to do what they do. Strictly speaking, a rock does not fall in order to hit the ground, and a river does not flow in order to reach the south.

Libertarians, however, are speaking not metaphorically but literally when they say that people act in order to achieve their purposes. After all, not even the most complex machine can act as a person does. A machine can break down and fail to operate, but only a human being can protest and stop work on purpose. In short, machines are caused to do what they do; people sometimes act for reasons, not from causes.

The upshot of the discussion is that the hard determinist, soft determinist, and libertarian agree partially and disagree partially with each of the other two. The hard determinist and soft determinist agree that determinism is true but disagree as to whether it is compatible with freedom. The hard determinist and libertarian agree that the two doctrines are incompatible but disagree as to which is true. The soft determinist and libertarian agree that people have free will but disagree as to whether freedom is compatible with determinism.

One of the three would appear to be correct and the other two wrong. But whose position is most persuasive? Each has a burden to bear.

Hard determinism has to overcome the plausible claim that, for instance, while attending a concert I have it within my power to applaud and also have it within my power not to applaud. The decision is up to me, but in that case I am free with regard to applauding, and hard determinism is refuted.

Soft determinism has to overcome the plausible claim that if my actions are the result of a causal claim extending back before my birth, then I am not free now with regard to any action. Thus determinism and free will are incompatible.

The libertarian has to overcome the plausible claim that every event is caused, whether a loud noise, a change in the weather, or a human action. If the events hadn't been caused, they wouldn't have occurred. Thus because determinism and free will are incompatible and determinism is true, free will is false.

But which position is correct? Just as each member of a jury at a trial needs to make a decision and defend a view after considering all the relevant evidence, so each philosophical inquirer needs to make a decision and defend a view after considering all the relevant arguments.

Granted, philosophical questions are perplexing, but to understand the difficulties is a significant step toward strengthening one's ability to think critically about fundamental issues. Anyone who supposes that a philosophical problem is easily solved probably hasn't fully understood the problem.

Notes

1 The following information is found in Irving Stone, *Clarence Darrow for the Defense* (Garden City, NY: Doubleday, Doran, 1941), 384–91.

2 *Attorney for the Damned*, ed. Arthur Weinberg (New York: Simon and Schuster, 1957), 37, 65.

3 Weinberg, 37.

4 The expressions "hard determinism" and "soft determinism" were coined by William James (1842–1910) in his essay "The Dilemma of Determinism," reprinted in *Essays on Faith and Morals* (Cleveland: World, 1962).

5 *The Maxims of La Rochefoucauld*, trans. Louis Kronenberger (New York: Random House, 1959), #379.

6 John Hospers, "What Means This Freedom?," *Determinism and Freedom in the Age of Modern Science*, ed. Sidney Hook (New York: Collier, 1961), 138.

7 For a detailed discussion of the philosophical implications of quantum mechanics, see Ernest Nagel, *The Structure of Science* (New York: Harcourt Brace Jovanovich, 1961), ch. 10.

8 A.S. Eddington, *The Nature of the Physical World* (New York: Macmillan, 1928), 342.

9 L. Susan Stebbing, *Philosophy and the Physicists* (New York: Dover, 1958), 51–52.

10 Sir Arthur Conan Doyle, *The Sign of Four*, in *The Complete Sherlock Holmes* (Garden City, NY: Doubleday, n.d.), 111.

5
Random Choices

An assumption common to all sides in the determinism and free will debate is that an action done for no reason is a senseless occurrence. I want to suggest, however, that a random choice can be undetermined yet purposeful.

The libertarian claim that the doctrine of free will can be true only if determinism is false has often been attacked on the grounds that "what is random is no more free than what is caused."[1] As A.J. Ayer (1910–89) argued:

> Either it is an accident that I choose to act as I do or it is not. If it is an accident, then it is merely a matter of chance that I did not choose otherwise; and if it is merely a matter of chance that I did not choose otherwise, it is surely irrational to hold me morally responsible for choosing as I did. But if it not an accident that I choose to do one thing rather than another, then presumably there is some causal explanation of my choice; and in that case we are led back to determinism.[2]

I want to call attention to a common phenomenon that has not often been the subject of philosophical concern but that on examination suggests that a random act, although seemingly uncaused, need be neither accidental nor irresponsible.

We are frequently called on to make a conscious choice from among alternatives that are equal in their degree of attractiveness. "Pick a card." "Choose a number from one to ten." "Park your car in any of the available spaces." "Have a cupcake." Normally none of us has any difficulty making such a random choice. Yet how do we manage to perform these seemingly simple tasks? How do we decide which card to pick or which number to choose?

At a party you are offered a plate of cookies. You select one, and the following conversation ensues:

Host: "Why did you choose that one?"
You: "You said, 'Take one.' So I did."
Host: "But why did you take that one?"
You: "I don't know. I just chose."

At the store you buy one box of corn flakes rather than another of the same brand and size, although they appear equally wholesome. In the park you sit on one bench rather than another, although others would serve equally well. While writing a philosophical paper you choose "Jones" as an example of a proper name, although "Smith" would be equally appropriate. None of these decisions causes you any anguish; they are made with ease.

Can such random choices be explained? Of course, we can explain a person's deciding to spend money on corn flakes rather than prunes, although some philosophers would say such an explanation is ultimately causal in nature, while others would say the appropriate explanation is irreducibly in terms of the agent's reasons or purposes. But can we explain a person's decision to buy one particular box of corn flakes rather than another?

On the one hand, to suppose that each time I am asked to choose a box of cereal a causal explanation can be provided as to why I picked a certain one is to adhere to determinism but to extrapolate wildly beyond available empirical data. On the other hand, to assume the choice can be explained in terms of my intentions is to be committed to the view that if we have no reason to prefer one choice to another, then we cannot choose at all. Yet we have no trouble making a random choice even in circumstances in which we find it impossible, before or after, to think of any basis to prefer one of the alternatives. Indeed, if we had to postpone such a choice until we could figure out a reason for our preference, our lives would come to a virtual standstill. Should I open this letter or that one first? Should I walk home this way or that?[3] Without the ability to make random choices, we would be caught in a nightmare of indecision.

I believe we possess the ability to make random choices. We are not condemned to the fate of Buridan's Ass, the animal featured in medieval debate who died while, equally pressed by hunger and thirst, he stood motionless midway between a bundle of hay and a pail of water. What we do in such a situation is make a random choice. Faced with equally attractive or unattractive alternatives, we are not bludgeoned into inactivity by some need for a decision principle. We simply choose. To refer to such a random choice as either accidental or irresponsible would surely be misleading.

P.H. Nowell-Smith (1914–2006) was thus mistaken when he equated a random occurrence with "an Act of God, or a miracle."[4] He even denied that such an occurrence could be an act at all, but, as we have seen, a random choice is an ordinary action that each of us performs frequently. Indeed, not only are random choices actions, they appear to be good candidates, although not the only ones, for membership in that class of actions we ordinarily designate as "free."

Notes

1 A.C. MacIntyre, "Determinism," *Mind* 66, no. 261 (1957), 30.

2 A.J. Ayer, *Philosophical Essays* (New York: St. Martin's Press, 1963), 275.

3 See William James's intriguing discussion of his choice whether to walk home by Divinity Avenue or Oxford Street in "The Dilemma of Determinism," 145–83.

4 P.H. Nowell-Smith, *Ethics* (Baltimore: Penguin, 1954), 282.

PART III: RELIGIOUS BELIEF

6

Philosophical Proofs and Religious Commitment

We turn now from concerns about human freedom to issues about religious belief. To begin, can the existence of God be proved philosophically? I myself don't think so, but, contrary to what many suppose, I do not find that such proofs are necessary or sufficient for religious commitment. In short, you might accept a philosophical proof of God's existence yet not belong to any religion, or you might reject all philosophical proofs for God's existence yet embrace a religion. Thus the possibilities are more varied than often supposed.

We start with a familiar question: Does God exist? A theist believes that God exists; an atheist believes that God does not exist; an agnostic believes that at present the matter is undecidable. Which of these positions is most reasonable?

The first step is to determine what is meant by the term "God." The word has been used in various ways, ranging from the Greek concept of the Olympian gods to the proposal by John Dewey (1859–1952) that the divine is the "active relation between ideal and actual."[1] Let us adopt the more usual view, common to many religious believers, that "God" refers to an all-good, all-powerful, all-knowing, eternal creator of the world. The question, then, is whether a being of that description exists.

Throughout the centuries, various philosophical arguments have been presented to prove the existence of God. They can be formulated and defended in a variety of ways, but I shall bypass innumerable complexities to focus on the basic structure of the three most discussed lines of reasoning.

We begin with the *cosmological argument*, which rests on the assumption that everything that exists depends for its existence on something else. For example, a house results from the actions of its builder, and rain results from certain meteorological conditions. But if everything that exists depends for its existence on something else, then the world itself depends for its existence on something else, and this "something else" is God.

Although the cosmological argument may seem initially plausible, it has a major difficulty, for if everything that exists depends for its existence on something else, then whatever the world's existence depends on also depends for its existence on something else. In that case, the world's existence would not depend on God, for God is an all-powerful being and thus does not depend on anything else for existence.

A defender of the cosmological argument might try to surmount this difficulty by claiming that whatever the world's existence depends on does not depend on something else but is self-explanatory, i.e., the reason for its existence lies within itself. If, however, we admit the possibility that something is self-explanatory, the cosmological argument is weakened, for if the world's existence depends on something that can be self-explanatory, why cannot the world itself be self-explanatory? In that case, no need would arise to assume something on which the existence of the world depends, because the existence of the world would be self-explanatory.

In an attempt to salvage the cosmological argument, a defender might argue that ultimately something must be responsible for everything, and this "something" is God. Yet even if we grant that something is responsible for everything (and this supposition could be contested by appeal to the mathematical notion of an infinite series), the "something" may not be all-good, all-powerful, all-knowing, or eternal. Perhaps the "something" is evil or ceased to exist after a brief life. No such possibilities are excluded by the cosmological argument, and thus most philosophers, although not all, do not find it successful.

A second classic proof for the existence of God is the *ontological argument*. It makes no appeal to empirical evidence but purports to demonstrate that God's essence implies God's existence. This argument has various versions, the best known of which share a basic structure. God is defined as the greatest conceivable being, one who possesses all perfections. Then assuming that a being who exists is greater than one who doesn't, God must exist; otherwise God would not be the greatest conceivable being.

Although this argument has been defended in subtle ways, it is open to the crucial criticism, stated succinctly by Immanuel Kant (1724–1804), that existence is not an attribute. In other words, the definition of anything remains the same whether that thing exists. For example, the definition of a unicorn would not be altered if we discovered a living unicorn, just as our definition of a whooping crane would not be altered if whooping cranes became extinct. In short, whether unicorns or whooping cranes exist does not affect the meaning of the terms "unicorn" and "whooping crane."

To clarify this point, imagine a ferocious tiger. Now imagine a ferocious tiger that exists. What more is imagined in the second case than the first? Our concept of a ferocious tiger remains the same whether any ferocious tigers exist.

Applying this insight to the ontological argument, we see what many philosophers, although again not all, believe is a serious weakness. Because the definition of something remains the same whether it exists, the definition of "God" remains the same whether God exists. Thus existence cannot be part of the definition of God. God may be defined as the greatest conceivable being, one who possesses every perfection, but existence does not render something greater, because existence is no attribute at all. To assert that something exists is not to ascribe greatness or perfection to the thing but to state a fact about the world. What we mean by "God" is one matter; whether God exists is another. The ontological argument conflates the two and thereby is in danger of going awry.

The third argument we shall consider, the *teleological argument*, is much less abstruse. Its defenders point out that the world possesses a highly ordered structure, just like an extraordinarily complex machine. Each part is adjusted to the other parts with wondrous precision. For instance, the human eye, which so many of us take for granted, is a mechanism of such intricacy that its design is breathtaking. But doesn't a design require a designer? The magnificent order of our world cannot be a result of chance but must be the work of a supreme mind responsible for the order. That supreme mind is God.

Although this argument has persuasive power, it suffers from several significant problems. To begin with, any world would exhibit some kind of order. Were you at random to drop ten coins on the floor, they would exhibit an order. An order, therefore, does not imply an orderer. If we use the term "design" to mean "a consciously established order," then a design implies a designer. But the crucial question is: does our world exhibit mere order or a design?

If the world were just like a machine, as the teleological argument claims, then because a machine has a design and a designer, so would the world. But is the world just like a machine? Hume, in his *Dialogues Concerning Natural Religion*, suggested that our experience is too limited for us to accept such an analogy. Philo, the skeptic in the *Dialogues*, notes that although the world bears some slight resemblance to a machine, the world is also similar to an animal: "A continuous circulation of matter in it produces no disorder: A continual waste in every part is incessantly repaired. The closest sympathy is perceived throughout the entire system: and each part or member, in performing its proper offices, operates both to its own preservation and to that of the whole."[2] Cleanthes, the rational theist in the *Dialogues*, adds that the world is also somewhat like a vegetable, because neither has sense organs or brain, although both exhibit life and movement.

The key point is that whereas any machine requires a designer, animals and vegetables come into being differently from machines.

Hume was not suggesting that the world came into being as does an animal or vegetable, but he wished to demonstrate that the world is not sufficiently like an animal, a vegetable, or a machine to permit us to draw reasonable conclusions from such weak analogies. Lacking them, the teleological argument is undermined, for we have no reason to believe that the world exhibits a design rather than mere order.

As Philo points out, however, even if we were to accept the analogy of world and machine, the argument still runs into difficulties. Let us grant, he says, that like effects prove like causes. Then if the world is like a machine, the cause of the world is like the cause of a machine. Remember, however, that machines are usually built after many trials, hence the world was probably built after many attempts. Machines are usually built by many workers, thus the world was probably built by many deities. Those who build machines are often inexperienced, careless, or foolish, so the gods, too, may be inexperienced, careless, or foolish. Perhaps this world "was only the first rude essay of some infant deity, who afterwards abandoned it, ashamed of his lame performance." Or perhaps "It is the work only of some dependent, inferior deity; and is the object of derision to his superiors." The world might even be "the production of old age and dotage in some superannuated deity; and ever since his death, has run on at adventures, from the first impulse and active force which it received from him."[3] By suggesting such possibilities Hume demonstrated that even if we grant an analogy between the world and a machine, and further agree that both were designed, we are not thereby committed to believing that the world's design is the work of one all-good, all-powerful, all-knowing eternal designer.

What, then, is the source of order? The world may have gone through innumerable structural changes until a stable pattern was reached, and the existence of such complex phenomena as the human eye may be a result of the process of natural selection whereby surviving forms of life are those than can adjust. Such an explanation of the world's order not only requires no recourse to the hypothesis of a supreme designer but has also been confirmed by biological research since the time of Charles Darwin.

I conclude, then, that none of the three best-known arguments for the existence of God, as I have presented them, is without flaws. Might a version of one of the arguments be rendered much more plausible than I have suggested? Some philosophers believe so, but rather than exploring a myriad of suggestions pro and con, let me consider a different question: Are religious believers deeply concerned with whether the existence of God can be proved by a philosophical argument? The evidence suggests they are not, and I want to explain why their attitude is reasonable.

Many might suppose that religious believers would be vitally interested in philosophical proofs for the existence of God, that when a proof of God's existence is persuasively defended, believers would be most enthusiastic and when a proof is refuted, they would be seriously disappointed. Such is not the case. Indeed, religious believers seem remarkably uninterested in the subject. They apparently consider discussion of such proofs to be an intellectual game with no relevance to religious belief or activity. For example, Søren Kierkegaard (1813–55) remarked, "Whoever therefore attempts to demonstrate the existence of God ... [is] an excellent subject for a comedy of the higher lunacy."[4]

In what follows I wish to explain why religious believers have so little interest in philosophical proofs for the existence of God, I believe this lack of concern is reasonable, and that whatever the philosophical significance of such proofs, they have little relevance to religion.

Suppose we assume, contrary to what most philosophers believe, that the three classic proofs for the existence of God are all sound. Let us grant the existence of the most perfect conceivable being who is the designer of the universe. What implications of this supposition would be relevant to our lives?

Some people would feel more secure in the knowledge that the world had been planned by an all-good being. Others would feel insecure, realizing the extent to which their existence depended on a decision of this being. In any case, most people, out of either fear or respect, would wish to act in accord with God's will.

Belief in God by itself, however, provides no hint whatsoever of which actions God wishes us to perform, or what we ought to do to please or obey God. We may affirm that God is all-good, yet have no way of knowing the highest moral standards. All we may presume is that, whatever these standards, God always acts in accordance with them. We might expect God to have implanted the correct moral standards in our minds, but this supposition is doubtful in view of the conflicts among people's intuitions. Furthermore, even if consensus prevailed, it might be only a means by which God tests us to see whether we have the courage to dissent from popular opinion.

Some would argue that if God exists, then murder is immoral, because it destroys what God with infinite wisdom created. This argument, however, appears to fail on several grounds. First, God also created germs, viruses, and disease-carrying rats. Because God created these things, ought they not be eliminated? Second, if God arranged for us to live, God also arranged for us to die. By killing, are we assisting the work of God? Third, God provided us with the mental and physical potential to commit murder. Does God wish us to fulfill this potential?

Thus God's existence alone does not appear to imply any particular moral precepts. We may hope our actions are in accord with God's standards, but no test is available to check whether what we do is best in God's eyes. Some good people suffer great ills, whereas some seemingly evil people achieve happiness. Perhaps in a future life these outcomes will be reversed, but we have no way of ascertaining who, if anyone, is ultimately punished and who ultimately rewarded.

Over the course of history, those who believed in God's existence typically were eager to learn God's will and tended to rely on those individuals who claimed to possess such insight. Diviners, seers, and priests were given positions of great influence. Competition among them was severe, though, for no one could be sure which oracle to believe.

In any case, prophets died, and their supposedly revelatory powers disappeared with them. For practical purposes, however, what was needed was a permanent record of God's will. This requirement was met by the writing of holy books in which God's will was revealed to all. But although many such books were supposed to embody the will of God, they conflicted with one another. Which was to be accepted? Belief in the existence of God by itself yields no answer.

I would suggest that the only direct, unmistakable avenue to the divine will is an experience in which one senses the presence of God and apprehends which, if any, of the putative holy books is genuine. To be certain, however, that you are experiencing God's presence and apprehending God's will, the experience cannot be open to error, for only then can it provide an unshakeable foundation for theistic belief. If one undergoes such an incorrigible experience, it guarantees which holy book is genuine and consequently which rituals, prayers, and actions God authorizes. Note, most importantly, that such an experience by itself validates the existence of God, for unless God's presence has been experienced, the message may not be true. Thus any further proof of God's existence is unnecessary.

For someone who does not undergo what is believed to be a genuine experience of the divine, several possibilities remain open. The individual may accept another person's claim to have had such an experience, thereby accepting any holy book that has been revealed and also accepting the existence of God, because unless this other person has experienced the presence of God, the report could be mistaken.

Suppose, however, that you do not accept someone else's report of an experience of God. This unwillingness may be due either to philosophical doubts concerning the possibility of such an experience or practical doubt that anyone has ever undergone such an experience. In either case adherence to a particular view of God's will seems to be unreasonable.

Not surprisingly, then, religious believers show less concern than might be expected about proofs for the existence of God. If the proof is sound, it merely confirms what is already known on the stronger evidence of someone's personal experience. If the proof is unsound, it does not undermine what is already known on the basis of such experience. In either case religious experience trumps philosophical proof.

Notes

1 John Dewey, *The Later Works of John Dewey*, 1925–1953, vol. 9, ed. Jo Ann Boydston (Carbondale: Southern Illinois University Press, 1988), 34.

2 David Hume, *Dialogues Concerning Natural Religion and Other Writings*, ed. Dorothy Coleman (New York: Cambridge University Press, 2007), pt. 6, par. 3.

3 Hume, pt. 5, par. 12.

4 Søren Kierkegaard, *Philosophical Fragments*, trans. David F. Swenson (Princeton: Princeton University Press, 1936), 3. 34.

7
The Theodicy Trap

Even if the philosophical proofs for the existence of God do not succeed, that result by itself fails to prove that God does not exist. To reach such a conclusion requires a separate argument, and a common one questions how evil can exist in a world created by a God who is all-knowing, all-powerful, and all-good. Here I consider this problem, explain a familiar reply to it, and consider a serious difficulty with that reply.

The world is beset by evils. Could it, therefore, have been created by an omnipotent, omni-benevolent God? Epicurus (341–270 BCE) thought not, and put the point succinctly: Is God willing to prevent evil, but not able? Then He is impotent. Is He able, but not willing? Then He is malevolent. Is He both able and willing? From where, therefore, comes evil?

This line of argument is commonly known as "the problem of evil," and developing a solution is the goal of theodicy, a term derived from the Greek words *theos* and *dike*, meaning "God" and "righteous." If a theodicy works, then it demonstrates at least that a world containing evil could have been the creation of an omnipotent, omni-benevolent God. But is that situation merely an unlikely possibility, or a probability? The most successful theodicy would show that the world's widespread evils should have been expected, given that the creator was omnipotent and omni-benevolent.

A theodicy is shaky if it explains only some evils but not all. For if certain evils are inconsistent with the existence of God, then their occurrence would disprove God's existence. Yet as experience makes all too clear, if evil is possible, then it likely has occurred or will occur. Thus a successful theodicy needs to offer a justification for all possible evils. Only then is theism secure.

Suppose, for example, an earthquake occurs, killing thousands. Some might suppose that such an event would undermine belief in an all-powerful, all-good creator of the world. With a successful theodicy in hand, however, theism would be safe from refutation by such an event; its occurrence could be explained without limiting the power or goodness of God.

No wonder, then, that theists have long sought a successful theodicy. Were this goal attained, however, it would lead into a trap. For if God's existence were compatible with all evils, why should belief in God afford any comfort?

For example, Psalm 23 refers to God as our shepherd. Even as "I walk through a valley of deepest darkness, I fear no harm, for You are with me."[1] But why shouldn't I fear harms? They may befall me even if I am in God's care.

Perhaps comfort is supposed to be found eventually in a next world, although that concept is obscure. As to this world, however, not only can good things happen to bad people, and bad things happen to good people, but the most wonderful things may happen to the worst people, and the most awful things may happen to the best people. A successful theodicy envisions and justifies all these possibilities.

That the world was designed by an omnipotent, omni-benevolent God might appear to be a basis for optimism. A successful theodicy, however, proves that God's plan could include every horrible occurrence imaginable, thus destroying any reason to be hopeful about events in this world.

Consider an analogous case. Suppose I recommend a restaurant, praising it for the excellence of its management. During your visit, though, you find the ambience gloomy, the service poor, the food unpalatable, and the cost high. When you express disappointment about your visit, I present an argument proving that all these conditions are consistent with the management's excellence. Indeed, I even show that such conditions are to be expected in a restaurant with excellent management. You may not know how to refute my argument, but the next time I recommend a restaurant on the basis of its excellent management, you won't be eager to eat there. After all, my argument that excellent management is consistent with an inferior dining experience implies that you have no reason to suppose that conditions at a restaurant with excellent management will be in any way satisfactory.

Similarly, if God's plan for the world is consistent with a succession of the worst evils, you have no reason to suppose that conditions in the world need ever be in any way satisfactory. A drought, for example, might persist for years, while a successful theodicy would provide a justification for the continuing oppressive condition. Moreover, praying to God for rain in those circumstances appears to make little sense, for if the draught is justified, why should God stop it?

To highlight this problem, consider the well-known theodicy offered by Richard Swinburne.[2] He assures us that God's plans require "much evil." Moral evils, those that human beings inflict on one another, are necessary for free will. Hence my suffering as a result of your freely chosen evil action is not entirely a loss for me, because I have contributed to the cause of freedom. "Those who are allowed to die for their country and thereby save their country from foreign oppression are privileged." Thus according to this theodicy, being the victim of injustice has a good side, even for the victim.

As for natural evils, those for which human beings are not responsible, Swinburne maintains that they give us the opportunity to perform worthy acts. Pain, for instance, helps develop patience. Therefore injustice contributes to the good not only as a by-product of free choice but also as an effective means for victims to develop moral virtue.

Swinburne's theodicy is so powerful that it implies not only that our world would be worse without evils but that heaven would be better if it contained them. In fact, Swinburne doesn't hesitate to draw this conclusion. He notes that heaven "lacks a few goods which our world contains, including the good of being able to reject the good."

Indeed, in reflecting on his theodicy, Swinburne warns: "I would not in most cases recommend that a pastor give this chapter to victims of sudden distress at their worst moment, to read for consolation. But this is not because its arguments are unsound; it is simply that most people in deep despair need comfort, not argument."

Swinburne recognizes that his theodicy offers no comfort. The crucial point, however, is that no successful theodicy does; it justifies whatever events occur.

The sad fate of some is to suffer through years filled with sorrow and suffering, anguish and agony, even tortures of mind and body. A successful theodicy, however, would demonstrate that such wretched lives, no matter how common, do not conflict with belief in an omnipotent, omni-benevolent God. If they did, then theism would fall prey to the problem of evil. A successful theodicy would solve that problem but leave believers without any reason to expect support from God.

In that connection, recall the moving words of the Levite benediction:

> "The Lord bless you and protect you!
> The Lord deal kindly and graciously with you!
> The Lord bestow His favor upon you and grant you peace!"[3]

A successful theodicy would prove that even with the Lord's blessing and protection, the Lord's kindness and graciousness, and the Lord's favor, your life on earth may be filled with evils, and you shouldn't expect God to alleviate them. After all, a successful theodicy has demonstrated that whatever evils occur, God views them as contributing to a greater good.

If this conclusion is unacceptable to theists, one way out would be to cease searching for a successful theodicy, instead continuing to conceive of God as omni-benevolent but recognizing God's power as limited. In that case, faced with a pandemic, for instance, theists could perhaps find some comfort in the realization that God wished to provide immediate relief but was unable to do so. Moreover, praying to God would still be appropriate, although God could not grant every request.

Admittedly this account of God's nature would likely appeal to few theists. By accepting it, however, they would escape having to defend the seemingly implausible claim made by every successful theodicy that God considers all evils, including all pandemics, to be enhancements of life.

Notes

1 Psalms 23:4. The translation is from *Tanakh: The Holy Scriptures* (Philadelphia: The Jewish Publication Society, 1988).

2 Richard Swinburne, *Is There a God?* (Oxford and New York: Oxford University Press, 1996), 96, 102, 113.

3 Numbers 6:24–26.

8
Religion without God

A common assumption is that religion depends on belief in a deity separate from the natural world. Yet various religions reject the concept of a supernatural God. These include Jainism, Theravada Buddhism, Mimamsa and Samkhya Hinduism, as well as Reconstructionist Judaism and "Death of God" versions of Christianity. In this chapter I explain how such options are possible.

I propose to show that nothing in the theory or practice of religion—not ritual, not prayer, not metaphysical belief, not moral commitment—necessitates a commitment to theism. In other words, just as you may believe in God yet not practice any religion, so you may be religious without believing in God.

Consider first the concept of a ritual. It is a prescribed symbolic action. In the case of religion, the ritual is prescribed by a religious organization and the act symbolizes some aspect of religious belief. If the religion is supernaturalistic (i.e., if it believes in a supernatural deity or deities), then those who reject such theology may as a result consider any ritual irrational. Yet although particular rituals may be based on irrational beliefs, nothing about the practice of ritual is inherently irrational.

Think of two people shaking hands when meeting. This act is a ritual, prescribed by our society and symbolic of the individuals' mutual respect. The act is in no way irrational. If people shook hands in order to ward off evil demons, then shaking hands would indeed be irrational. That reason, however, is not why people shake hands. The ritual may have originated as a gesture of peace indicating that the proffered hand is without a weapon. Regardless, the ritual has no connection with God, demons, or weapons, but now indicates the respectful attitude one person has toward another.

Some might assume that the ritual of handshaking escapes irrationality only because the ritual is not prescribed by any specific organization and is not part of an elaborate ceremony. To see that this assumption is false, consider the graduation ceremony at a college. The graduates and faculty members all wear peculiar hats and robes, and the participants stand and sit at appropriate times. The ceremony, however, is not at all irrational. Indeed, the rites of graduation day, far from being irrational, are symbolic of commitment to the process of education and the life of reason.

At first glance, rituals may seem a comparatively insignificant feature of life, yet they are a pervasive and treasured aspect of human experience. Who would want to eliminate the festivities associated with holidays such as New Year's Day or Thanksgiving? What would college football be without songs, cheers, flags, and the innumerable other symbolic features surrounding the game? Even those who disdain popular rituals typically proceed to establish their own distinctive ones, such as characteristic habits of dress that symbolize a rejection of traditional mores.

Religious persons, like all others, search for an appropriate means of emphasizing their commitment to a group or its values. Rituals provide such a means. Granted, supernaturalistic religion has often fused its rituals with superstition, but nonreligious rituals can be equally superstitious. For instance, most Americans view the Fourth of July as an occasion on which they can express pride in their country's heritage. With this purpose in mind, the holiday is one of great significance. If, however, the singing of the fourth verse of "The Star-Spangled Banner" four times on the Fourth of July were thought to protect the country against future disasters, then the original meaning of the holiday would be lost in a maze of superstition.

A naturalistic (i.e., non-supernaturalistic) religion need not utilize ritual in a superstitious manner, because such a religion does not employ rituals to please a benevolent deity or appease an angry one. Rather, naturalistic religion views rituals, in the words of Rabbi Jack J. Cohen (1919–2012), as "the enhancement of life through the dramatization of great ideals."[1] If a group stresses justice or freedom, why should the group not utilize ritual in order to emphasize these goals? Such a use of ritual serves to solidify the group and strengthen its devotion to its expressed purposes. These are buttressed if the ritual in question has the force of tradition, having been performed by many generations who have belonged to the same group and struggled to achieve the same goals. Ritual so conceived is not a form of superstition but a reasonable means of strengthening religious commitment, as useful to naturalistic as to supernaturalistic religion.

Let us next turn to the concept of prayer. Some might suppose that naturalistic religion could have no use for prayer, because prayer is supposedly addressed to a supernatural being, and proponents of naturalistic religion do not believe in the existence of such a being. This objection, however, oversimplifies the concept of prayer, focusing attention on one type while neglecting an equally important but different sort.

Supernaturalistic religion makes extensive use of petitionary prayer—that is, prayer that asks favors from a supernatural being. These may range from the personal happiness of the petitioner to the general welfare of society. Because petitionary prayer rests on the assumption that a supernatural being exists, such prayer clearly has no place in a naturalistic religion.

Not all prayers, however, are prayers of petition. Some prayers are prayers of meditation. These are not directed to any supernatural being and are not requests for granting favors. Rather, these prayers provide the opportunity for persons to rethink their fundamental commitments and rededicate themselves to their ideals. Such prayers may take the form of silent devotion or involve oral repetition of central texts. Just as Americans repeat the Pledge of Allegiance and reread the Gettysburg Address, so adherents of naturalistic religion repeat the statement of their ideals and reread the documents that embody their traditional beliefs.

Granted, supernaturalistic religions, to the extent that they utilize prayers of meditation, tend to treat these prayers irrationally by supposing that if the prayers are not uttered a precise number of times under certain specific conditions, then the prayers lose all value. Yet prayer need not be viewed in this way. Rather, as biologist Sir Julian Huxley (1887–1975) wrote, prayer "permits the bringing before the mind of a world of thought which in most people must inevitably be absent during the occupation of ordinary life ... [I]t is the means by which the mind may fix itself upon this or that noble or beautiful or awe-inspiring idea, and so grow to it and come to realize it more fully."[2]

Such a use of prayer may be enhanced by song, instrumental music, and various types of symbolism. These elements fused together provide the means for adherents of naturalistic religion to engage in religious services akin to those engaged in by adherents of supernaturalistic religion. The difference between the two services is that those who participate in the latter come to relate themselves to God, whereas those who participate in the former come to relate themselves to their fellow human beings and the world in which we live.

Thus far we have examined how ritual and prayer can be utilized in naturalistic religion, but to adopt a religious perspective also involves metaphysical beliefs and moral commitments. Can these be maintained without recourse to supernaturalism?

If we use the term "metaphysics" in its usual sense, referring to the systematic study of the most basic features of existence, then a metaphysical system may be either supernaturalistic or naturalistic. Representative of a supernaturalistic theory are René Descartes (1596–1640) and Gottfried Leibniz (1646–1716). Representative of a naturalistic theory are Baruch Spinoza (1632–77) and John Dewey. Spinoza's *Ethics*, for example, one of the greatest of metaphysical works, explicitly rejects the view that any being exists apart from Nature itself. Spinoza identifies God with Nature as a whole and urges that the good life consists in coming to understand Nature. In his words, "our salvation, or blessedness, or freedom consists in a constant and eternal love toward God."[3] Spinoza's concept of God, however, is explicitly not supernaturalistic, and Spinoza's metaphysical system thus exemplifies not only a naturalistic metaphysics but also the possibility of reinterpreting the concept of God within a naturalistic framework.

Can those who do not believe in a supernaturalistic God commit themselves to moral principles, or is the acceptance of moral principles dependent on the acceptance of supernaturalism? Some have assumed that those who reject a supernaturalistic God are necessarily immoral, for their denial of the existence of God leaves them free to act without fear of divine punishment. This assumption, however, appears mistaken.

A strong reply to the view that morality must rest on belief in a supernatural God was provided more than two thousand years ago by Plato (c. 429–347 BCE) in his remarkable dialogue *Euthyphro*. Plato's teacher, Socrates (469–399 BCE), who in most of Plato's works is given the leading role, asks the overconfident Euthyphro whether actions are right because God says they are right, or whether God says actions are right because they are right.

In other words, Socrates is inquiring whether actions are right because of God's fiat or whether God is subject to moral standards. If actions are right because of God's command, then anything God commands would be right. Had God commanded adultery, stealing, and murder, then adultery, stealing, and murder would be right—surely an unsettling and to many an unacceptable conclusion.

Granted, some may be willing to adopt this discomforting view, but then they face another difficulty. If the good is whatever God commands, then how can God be praised for issuing good commands? After all, they would be good whatever their content. In that case, the possibility of meaningfully praising the goodness of God seems to be lost.

The lesson here appears to be that might does not make right, even if the might is the infinite might of God. To act morally is neither to act out of fear of punishment nor to act as one is commanded.

Rather, it is to act as one ought to act, and how one ought to act is not dependent on anyone's power, even if the power be divine.

In that case actions are not right because God commands them; on the contrary, God commands them because they are right. What is right is independent of what God commands, for to be right, what God commands must conform to an independent standard.

We could act intentionally in accord with this standard without believing in the existence of God; therefore morality does not rest on that belief. Consequently those who do not believe in God can be highly moral (as well as immoral) people, and those who do believe in the existence of God can be highly immoral (as well as moral) people. This conclusion should come as no surprise to anyone who has contrasted the benevolent life of the Buddha (c. 563–c. 483 BCE), the inspiring teacher and atheist, with the malevolent life of the monk Tomás de Torquemada (1420–98), who devised and enforced the boundless cruelties of the Spanish Inquisition.

We have now seen that naturalistic religion is a genuine possibility, because reasonable individuals may perform rituals, utter prayers, accept metaphysical beliefs, and commit themselves to moral principles without believing in supernaturalism. Indeed, even Judaism or Christianity may be reinterpreted to eliminate any commitment to supernaturalism.

Here, for example, is how Rabbi Mordecai M. Kaplan (1881–1983), the founder of Reconstructionist Judaism, which rejects supernaturalism, responded to a skeptic who asked why, if the Bible isn't taken literally, Jews should nevertheless observe the Sabbath: "We observe the Sabbath not so much because of the account of its origin in Genesis, as because of the role it has come to play in the spiritual life of our People and of mankind.... The Sabbath day sanctifies our life by what it contributes to making us truly human and helping us to transcend those instincts and passions that are part of our heritage from the sub-human."[4]

And here from one of the major figures in the Christian "Death of God" movement, the Anglican Bishop of Woolwich John A.T.

Robinson (1919–83), who denied the existence of a God "up there" or "out there," is an account of the Holy Communion: "[T]oo often ... it ceases to be the holy meal, and becomes a religious service in which we turn our backs on the common and the community and in individualistic devotion go to 'make our communion' with 'the God out there.' This is the essence of the religious perversion, when worship becomes a realm into which to withdraw from the world to 'be with God'—even if it is only in order to receive strength to go back into it. In this case the entire realm of the non-religious (in other words, 'life') is relegated to the profane ..."[5]

Furthermore, a naturalistic religion can also be developed without deriving it from a supernaturalistic religion. Consider, for example, the views of Charles Frankel (1917–79), an opponent of supernaturalism, who nevertheless believed that religion, shorn of irrationality, can make a distinctive contribution to human life, providing deliverance from vanity, triumph over meanness, and endurance in the face of tragedy. As he put it, "it seems to me not impossible that a religion could draw the genuine and passionate adherence of its members while it claimed nothing more than to be poetry in which men might participate and from which they might draw strength and light."[6]

Such naturalistic options are philosophically respectable. Whether to choose any of them is for each person to decide.

Notes

1 Jack J. Cohen, *The Case for Religious Naturalism* (New York: Reconstructionist Press, 1958), 150.

2 Julian Huxley, *Religion without Revelation* (New York: New American Library, 1957), 141.

3 Baruch Spinoza, *Ethics*, ed. James Gutmann (New York: Hafner, 1957), pt. 5, prop. 36, note.

4 Mordecai M. Kaplan, *Judaism without Supernaturalism* (New York: Reconstructionist Press, 1958), 115–16.

5 John A.T. Robinson, *Honest to God* (Philadelphia: Westminster, 1963), 86–87.

6 Charles Frankel, *The Love of Anxiety and Other Essays* (New York: Harper & Row, 1965), 192.

PART IV: ETHICS

9 Moral Judgments

The terms "ethics" and "moral philosophy" may be used interchangeably. "Ethics" is derived from the Greek word "ethos" meaning "character"; "moral" is from the Latin "moralis," relating to "custom." A primary question in this area of philosophy is the source of ethical claims. Are they matters of fact or expressions of feelings? Let us consider the issue.

Some people believe that just as we are subject to scientific laws, such as that water freezes at zero degrees centigrade and boils at one hundred degrees Celsius, so murder is wrong and honesty is right. Moreover, just as laws of nature apply at any time and in any place, so do moral laws. The only difference is that laws of nature are tested by scientific method, while moral laws are tested by conscience.

This theory, however, runs into troubles. First, moral laws can be broken, whereas scientific laws cannot. A person can steal a book, thereby breaking a moral law, but cannot succeed in tossing a book into the air and prevent its being subject to the law of gravity. Second, the dictates of one person's conscience may conflict with those of another. How can we decide between them? We can appeal to the dictates of our own conscience, but ours may be biased. Or we can appeal to the dictates of the conscience of the majority, but theirs may also be mistaken. After all, moral principles are not decided by vote. Perhaps, then, moral judgments aren't true or false but merely express preferences. Yet almost all of us, faced with social injustice, argue to demonstrate its unfairness. Therefore reasoning does appear to have a role in arriving at conclusions about right and wrong.

Given this impasse, how to proceed? I suggest seeking to understand the nature of moral judgments by considering first some value claims unrelated to ethics. For instance, we speak of "a good car" or "bad television reception." How are these statements justified?

Suppose you are a member of a softball league. Your friend Beth tells you that Susan is an excellent ballplayer, so you ask her to join your team, but she turns out to be woefully inadequate. She drops balls thrown to her, misplays ground balls, and strikes out almost every time she comes to bat. You tell Beth that her recommendation of Susan was a mistake. Either Beth does not know how to judge a good ballplayer, or someone has misled her about Susan's abilities, because obviously Susan is not a good ballplayer.

When you say so, you are neither appealing to the dictates of conscience nor expressing an arbitrary preference. Rather, you are basing your judgment on the facts—facts about softball, not facts about goodness. The reason Susan is not a good ballplayer is that she hits poorly and fields inadequately. To defend your view, all you need do is point to Susan's batting and fielding averages. While disagreement may persist if Susan hits .250 and commits a few errors, without doubt a ballplayer who hits .150 and commits errors in every game is not a good ballplayer, whereas one who hits .350 and rarely commits an error is a good ballplayer. The distinction is clear, despite the possibility of borderline cases, just as the distinction between bald and hirsute is clear despite disputable instances.

Note that if Susan hits and fields well, someone would be confused to wonder if Susan might still lack one attribute essential to a good ballplayer, namely goodness, because if Susan hits and fields well, then she is a good ballplayer. Goodness is not another attribute besides hitting and fielding well but a shorthand way of referring to those skills.

Suppose when you tell Beth that Susan is not a good ballplayer, Beth agrees that Susan doesn't hit or field well, but Beth argues that a good ballplayer is one who is obliging to fans. She claims that because Susan has this attribute, she is a good ballplayer.

While Beth's reply would be exasperating, you could respond by emphasizing that the criteria of a good ballplayer are not arbitrary.

You play softball to win; hence good players are those who help in winning. Susan does not do so and therefore is not a good ballplayer.

If Beth thinks players who are obliging to fans help the team win, her view can be disproven by an appeal to the record books. But if Beth believes softball is played not to win but to gain popularity, then players who are obliging to fans may be more effective in achieving that aim. In such a case, however, Beth's recommendations of ballplayers would be of no value to the overwhelming number of participants whose aim in playing the game is to score more runs than the opposition.

We have extended this example far enough to clarify the nature of non-moral value judgments. First, although the term "good" is a commendation, the criteria for its use vary depending on the context and our purposes. Good apples, good computers, and good ballplayers are good for different reasons. Second, if two people disagree about a value judgment but agree on the criteria for goodness, then the disagreement is in principle resolvable by the use of empirical testing procedures. Third, if the two individuals disagree about a value judgment and also disagree on the criteria for goodness, then the two need to consider why they have chosen their differing criteria. If the people can find a basis for agreement on further ends that are supposed to justify the criteria, then the disagreement is again in principle resolvable by the use of empirical testing procedures. If, however, the ends are fundamentally incompatible, then the disagreement will not yield to rational resolution.

An obvious question is: What are the chances that in a moral disagreement the disputants will agree on ends? At first glance, searching for consensus might appear hopeless, but it may be found by recognizing that we depend on others to achieve our most valuable goals. As Jonathan Harrison (1924–2014) observed,

> We cannot conceive of a being like ourselves, who desires his own happiness, and the happiness of his family and friends (if

> not the happiness of the whole of mankind), who needs the company of his fellows, who is easily injured by their hostile acts, and who cannot continue to exist unless they co-operate with him—we cannot conceive of a being such as this approving of promise-breaking, dishonesty, and deliberate callousness to the interests of others.[1]

In short, our humanity requires that we rely on others, and therefore we approve of actions that facilitate cooperation.

Any individual who rejects this way of thinking and instead favors persecution and cruelty for their own sake is not to be argued with but to be guarded against. Interestingly, no political leader has ever come to power by promising to increase hatred, violence, and oppression. To gain public support, even the worst of dictators mouths the usual moral sentiments.

Thus if a moral skeptic should inquire why we should be concerned about the welfare of others, we can do no better than offer the response James Rachels (1941–2003) provided: "The reason one ought not to do actions that would hurt other people is: other people would be hurt. The reason one ought to do actions that would benefit other people is: other people would be benefitted." If such considerations count for nothing, then the discussion is over. But what if someone insistently maintains a position in favor of immorality? Then, quoting Rachels again, "he is saying something quite extraordinary. He is saying that he has no affection for friends or family, that he never feels pity or compassion, that he is the sort of person who can look on scenes of human misery with complete indifference, so long as he is not the one suffering.... Indeed, a man without any sympathy would scarcely be recognizable as a man."[2] The upshot is that a commitment to immorality is likely to be defended only by someone trying to make a theoretical point, who nevertheless expects to receive considerate treatment from others.

In sum, moral judgments, except for the most bedrock, are supported by facts, while depending on shared feelings. Thus ethical and scientific claims are in some ways similar and in some ways not. In both cases, however, the most effective means of assessing claims is by the use of reason.

Notes

1 Jonathan Harrison, "Empiricism in Ethics," *Philosophical Quarterly* 2:9 (1952), 306.

2 James Rachels, "Egoism and Moral Scepticism," in Steven M. Cahn, *A New Introduction to Philosophy* (New York: Harper & Row, 1971), 432–33.

10
Moral Principles

Many thinkers have tried to discover one supreme moral principle that in every situation indicates which course of action is morally correct and which incorrect. Can such a touchstone be found? In this chapter I consider the most plausible candidates.

In our search for a supreme moral principle, let us begin with a principle common to many religious traditions: the Golden Rule. Its positive formulation, attributed to Jesus, is: "In everything do to others as you would have them do to you."[1] The negative formulation, which appeared at least five centuries earlier, is attributed to Confucius (551–479 BCE) and was later proposed by the Jewish sage Hillel (110 BCE–10 CE). The latter put it as follows: "What is hateful to you, do not to your neighbor."[2] Is either of these the supreme moral principle?

Consider first the positive formulation. Granted, we usually should treat others as we would wish them to treat us. For instance, we should go to the aid of any injured person, just as we would wish that person to come to our aid if we were injured. If we always followed this rule, however, the results would be unfortunate. Masochists, for instance, derive pleasure from being hurt. Were they to act according to the principle in question, their duty would be to inflict pain, thereby doing to others as they wish done to themselves. Similarly, consider a person who enjoys receiving telephone calls, regardless of who is calling. The principle would require that person to telephone everyone, thereby reciprocating preferred treatment. Indeed, to fulfill the positive formulation of the Golden Rule would be impossible, because we wish so many to do much for us that we would not have time to do all that is necessary to treat them likewise. As Walter Kaufman (1921–80) commented, "anyone who tried to live up to Jesus' rule would become an insufferable nuisance."[3]

In this respect, the negative formulation of the Golden Rule is preferable, because it does not imply that we have innumerable duties toward everyone else. Neither does it imply that masochists ought to inflict pain on others, nor that those who enjoy receiving telephone calls ought themselves to make calls. While the negative formulation does not require these actions, however, neither does it forbid them. It enjoins us not to do to others what is hateful to ourselves, but pain is not hateful to the masochist and calls are not hateful to the telephone enthusiast. Thus because the negative formulation does not prohibit actions that ought to be prohibited, it is not the rule we are seeking.

Let us next sketch two other standards of conduct, each of which has sometimes been thought to be the supreme moral principle. One was originally formulated by Kant, who argued that the moral worth of an action should be judged not by its consequences but by the nature of the maxim (the principle) that motivates the action. Right actions are not therefore necessarily those with favorable consequences but those performed from the duty of acting in accord with correct maxims. But which maxims are correct? According to Kant, only those that can serve as universal laws, because they are applicable without exception to every person at any time. In other words, you should act only a maxim that can be universalized without contradiction (inconsistency).

To see what Kant had in mind, consider a specific example he used to illustrate his view. Suppose you need to borrow money, but it will be lent to you only if you promise to pay it back. Are you permitted to promise to repay the money, knowing you will not keep the promise? Kant proposed that the way to determine whether such an action is permissible is to universalize the maxim in question and see whether doing so leads to contradiction. The maxim is: "When

I believe myself to be in need of money, I will borrow money and promise to repay it, although I know I shall never be able to do so." Can this maxim be universalized without contradiction? Kant argued that it cannot. "For the universality of a law which says that anyone who believes himself to be in need could promise what he pleased with the intention of not fulfilling it would make the promise itself and the end to be accomplished by it impossible; no one would believe what was promised to him but would only laugh at such assertion as vain pretense."[4]

In other words, to make promises with no intention of keeping them would lead to the destruction of the practice of promising. Thus because the maxim in question cannot be universalized without contradiction, that maxim is not morally acceptable and, consequently, any action it motivates is immoral. According to Kant, then, the supreme moral principle is: "Act only according to that maxim by which you can at the same time will that it should become a universal law."

This principle, unfortunately seems to prohibit actions that should be permitted. Although we might agree that the maxim of making insincere promises cannot be universalized, we can easily imagine cases in which a person ought to make a promise without any intention of keeping it. Suppose, for example, you and your family will starve to death unless you obtain food immediately, and a wealthy person offers to provide the food if you will promise repayment within twenty-four hours. Surely we would say, contrary to Kant's principle, under these circumstances you ought to act on a maxim that cannot be universalized and make a promise you have no intention of keeping.

Kant's insistence that proper maxims admit no exceptions led him not only to disapprove actions that are appropriate but also to approve some that appear incompatible. Maxims he accepted may conflict, and in that case adherence to one involves the violation of another. In the preceding example, for instance, were you to act in accord with the maxim of never making insincere promises, you would violate another maxim affirmed by Kant, that of aiding those who are in distress. He argued that both maxims admit no exceptions, but because always abiding by both is impossible, Kant's position is problematic.

Perhaps his proposal raises difficulties because it concentrates exclusively on the motive for an action and fails to take its results into account. Hence let us next consider a principle that focuses on consequences, one defended by John Stuart Mill. He was a leading advocate for the ethical position known as *utilitarianism*, according to which an action is right insofar as it promotes the happiness of humanity and wrong in so far as it promotes unhappiness. By the term *happiness* Mill meant pleasure and the absence of pain. By *humanity* he meant all persons, each valued equally. Thus Mill's supreme moral principle is: Act in such a way as to produce the greatest pleasure for the greatest number of people, each person's pleasure counting equally.

This principle avoid the pitfalls of Kant's view, for whereas Kant admitted no exceptions to moral rules and seemingly was thus led to condemn insincere promises that saved human lives, the utilitarian principle is flexible enough to allow for any exceptions that increase overall happiness. Although Mill would agree that insincere promises are usually wrong, because they are apt to cause more pain than pleasure, he would allow that in some cases, such as that of the starving family, an insincere promise is morally justifiable, as it would tend to greater overall happiness than any alternative.

The flexibility of the utilitarian principle is advantageous but questionable, for it apparently permits actions that should be prohibited. Consider, for example, inhabitants of a city who each week abduct a stranger and place the unfortunate person in an arena to wrestle a lion. When the inhabitants of the city are challenged to justify this practice, they reply that although one person suffers much pain, thousands of spectators obtain greater pleasure from this form of entertainment than from any other, so the spectacle is justified on utilitarian grounds. Thus Mill's principle appears to yield an unacceptable implication. Other cases along similar lines likewise suggest the laxity of utilitarianism. The sheriff who hangs an innocent person to satisfy the vengeance of the townspeople may maximize pleasure but nevertheless acts immorally. Also unethical is the teacher who awards all students A's to maximize their pleasure and avoid causing anyone pain.

One way to try to salvage the utilitarian principle is to argue that not all pleasures are of equal quality; that, for instance, the pleasure of spectators at a lion arena is less valuable than that enjoyed by those at a piano recital. As Mill wrote, "It is better to be a human being dissatisfied than a pig satisfied; better to be Socrates dissatisfied than a fool satisfied. And if the fool, or the pig, are of a different opinion, it is because they only know their own side of the question. The other party to the comparison knows both sides."[5]

This move is dubious. Some individuals, knowing both sides of the question, would prefer to witness a struggle between human and lion rather than between human and keyboard. Even if only one knowledgeable individual has such taste, why should that person's view be disregarded? Furthermore, Mill's principle cannot be salvaged by the claim that attendance at a piano recital develops sensitivity whereas a visit to a lion arena dulls it, for, according to utilitarianism, actions are good to the extent that they produce pleasure, not to the extent that they produce sensitivity.

Perhaps given the complexities of the human condition, any search for a supreme moral principle is doomed to failure, but the analysis so far, even while omitting innumerable clarifications, qualifications, and countermoves, has at least succeeded in calling attention to one fundamental feature of morality. The positive and negative formulations of the Golden Rule, the Kantian principle, and utilitarianism all serve as reminders that a moral person is obligated to be sensitive to others. This insight motivates not only the biblical injunction to treat our fellow human beings as we wish to be treated, but also the utilitarian insistence that each person's happiness is to count neither more nor less than another's. The same theme is central to Kant's view, a point he made explicit by claiming that the supreme moral principle can be reformulated as follows: "Act so that you treat humanity, whether in your own person or in that of another, always as an end and never as a means only."[6] In short, the moral point of view involves taking into account interests apart from our own.

The claim has been made, though, that all human actions are motivated by selfishness. According to this theory, known as *psychological egoism*, all actions are attempts to enhance the agent's own pleasure. In other words, I am kind to others only to benefit myself.

An obvious response to this claim is to present cases in which people act unselfishly, such as a physician who lives among the poor to provide them with health care. The defender of psychological egoism responds, however, by asserting that the doctor derives pleasure from giving help and thus is acting selfishly after all.

The appropriate reply to this dubious line of argument was provided by P.H. Nowell-Smith: "To be selfish is not to do what one wants to do or enjoys doing, but to be hostile or indifferent to the welfare of others."[7] In other words, an unselfish person cares about others, whereas a selfish person does not. Whether an action is selfish does not depend on whether someone wants to do it but on what that person wants to do. If the point is to assist others, then the action is unselfish.

Still one might ask why we should act unselfishly. Why not just appear to be moral rather than actually being moral? Perhaps the best answer was provided by Hume: "[K]naves, with all their pretended cunning and abilities, [are] betrayed by their own maxims; and while they purpose to cheat with moderation and secrecy, a tempting incident occurs—nature is frail, and they give in to the snare, whence they can never extricate themselves without a total loss of reputation and the forfeiture of all future trust and confidence with mankind."[8]

In brief, immoral action is always a threat to one's self-interest, and rarely can this threat be minimized sufficiently to render the risk rational. But if someone decides to take a chance on unethical behavior, can we reason further with that individual? At least we can recall the words of La Rochefoucauld: "To virtue's credit we must confess that our greatest misfortunes are brought about by vice."[9] Thus even when sympathy is missing, morality rests on practicality.

Notes

1 Matthew 7:12, *The Holy Bible: New Revised Standard Version* (New York and Oxford: Oxford University Press, 1989).

2 Shabbath, 31a, *The Babylonian Talmud* (London: Soncino Press, 1938).

3 Walter Kaufman, *The Faith of a Heretic* (New York: Doubleday, 1963), 212.

4 Immanuel Kant, *Foundations of the Metaphysics of Morals*, 2nd ed., trans. Lewis White Beck (Saddle River, NJ: Prentice-Hall, 1997), 38–39.

5 John Stuart Mill, *Utilitarianism* (Indianapolis: Hackett, 1979), 10.

6 Kant, 46.

7 P. H. Nowell-Smith, *Ethics* (Baltimore: Penguin Books, 1954), 142–43.

8 David Hume, *An Enquiry Concerning the Principles of Morals* (New York: Liberal Arts Press, 1957), 103.

9 *The Maxims of La Rochefoucauld*, #379.

11
Moral Puzzles

Philosophers often use brief puzzles to raise serious issues. Here are three moral perplexities that I offer for your consideration.

A. The Bus Puzzle

Some years ago, while riding a bus in New York City, I saw two men board, sit down, and find on their seat a package of gloves that appeared to have been newly purchased. After some discussion, one man indicated that he intended to keep the gloves for himself. An older fellow across the aisle, listening to the conversation, told the two that they should give the gloves to the bus driver, who would take them to the lost-and-found. This older man further explained that whoever had paid for the gloves would want them returned. Indeed, he claimed that taking the gloves under those circumstances would be stealing. In response, the two men insisted that they still intended to keep the gloves.

Moments later, the older man rose to leave the bus. As he passed the two others, he grabbed the package, gave the gloves to the driver, and hurried off.

What the bus driver did with the package I do not know. Perhaps he gave the gloves to the lost-and-found, contributed them to a relief organization, or returned them to the first two men. He might even have kept them for himself.

Whatever the outcome, given these circumstances, how should we morally assess the behavior of the two men who found the package, as well as the words and actions of the older man and the possible plans of the bus driver?

B. The Divestiture Puzzle

Suppose I hold one hundred shares of stock in a company that has embarked on a policy I consider immoral. I, therefore, wish to divest myself of those one hundred shares. For me to sell them, however, someone must buy them. But the buyer would be purchasing one hundred shares of "tainted" stock, and I would have abetted the buyer in this immoral course of action. Granted, the prospective buyer might not believe the stock tainted, but that consideration would be irrelevant to me, because I am convinced that, knowingly or unknowingly, the buyer would be doing what is immoral. Surely I should not take any steps that would assist or encourage the buyer in such deplorable conduct. Nor should I try to release myself from a moral predicament by entangling someone else. How, then, is principled divestiture possible?

C. The Happiness Puzzle

Joan earned a doctoral degree from a first-rate university and sought appointment to a tenure-track position in which she could teach and pursue her research. Unfortunately, she received no offers and was about to accept nonacademic employment when an unexpected call came inviting her for an interview at a highly attractive school. During her visit she was told by the Dean that the job was hers, subject to one condition. She was expected to teach a particular course each year in which numerous varsity athletes would enroll, and she would be required to award them all passing grades even if their work was in every respect unsatisfactory. Only the Dean would know of this special arrangement.

Joan rejected the position on moral grounds and continued trying to obtain a suitable opportunity in academic life. Never again, however, was she offered a faculty position, and she was forced to pursue a career path that gave her little satisfaction. Her potential as a teacher went unfulfilled, and her planned research was left undone. Throughout her life she remained embittered.

Kate also earned a doctoral degree from a first-rate university and sought appointment to a tenure-track position in which she could teach and pursue her research. She, too, received no offers and reluctantly was about to accept nonacademic employment when an unexpected call came inviting her for an interview at the same school Joan had visited. The Dean made Kate the identical offer that had been made to Joan. After weighing the options, Kate accepted the appointment, even though she recognized that doing so would require her to act unethically.

Kate went on to a highly successful academic career, became a popular teacher and renowned researcher, moved to a prestigious university, and enjoyed all the perquisites attendant to her membership on that school's renowned faculty. When on rare occasions she recalled the conditions of her initial appointment, she viewed the actions she had taken as an unfortunate but necessary step on her path to a wonderful life.

Joan acted morally but lived unhappily ever after, whereas Kate acted immorally but lived happily ever after. Thus I leave you with this dilemma: Which of the two was the wiser?

PART V: WELL-BEING

12
Living Well

What is the nature of a good life? Presumably it requires being a moral person, but what else is involved? I co-authored an earlier version of this chapter with Christine Vitrano, Associate Professor of Philosophy at Brooklyn College of The City University of New York. Here you find our answer, with which some philosophers agree and others do not, a familiar situation.

The legal philosopher Ronald Dworkin (1931–2013) urged that we should all seek to live well so as to achieve "successful" lives and avoid "wasted" ones. But does one model fit all? On this important point Dworkin wavered. He maintained that "there is, independently and objectively, a right way to live."[1] Yet he also recognized "the responsibility of each person to decide for himself ethical questions about which kinds of lives are appropriate and which would be degrading for him."[2]

What sort of life did Dworkin find degrading? We are not told but suspect that for such a successful academic, a degrading life might have been one without intellectual striving, just as a famed athlete might find to be degrading a life as a couch potato.

But what sorts of lives are worthy? To help answer the question, consider the following two fictional, though realistic, cases.

1. Pat received a bachelor's degree from a prestigious college, earned a PhD in philosophy from a leading university, was awarded an academic position at a first-rate school, and eventually earned tenure there. Pat is the author of numerous books, articles, and reviews, is widely regarded as a leading scholar and teacher, and is admired by colleagues and students for fairness and helpfulness. Pat is happily married, has two children, enjoys playing

bridge and the cello, and vacations each summer in a modest house on Cape Cod. Physically and mentally healthy, Pat is in good spirits, looking forward to years of continued happiness.

2. Lee did not attend college. After graduation from high school, Lee moved to a beach community in California and is devoted to sunbathing, swimming, and surfing. Lee has never married but has experienced numerous romances. Having inherited wealth from deceased parents, Lee has no financial needs but spends money freely on magnificent homes, luxury cars, the latest in electronic equipment, designer clothes, meals in fine restaurants, golfing holidays, and trips to far-flung locations. Lee has many friends and is admired for honesty and kindness. Physically and mentally healthy, Lee is in good spirits, looking forward to years of continued happiness.

Both Pat and Lee live in ways that appear to suit them. Both enjoy prosperity, treat others with respect, engage in activities they find fulfilling, and report they are happy. So are both living well? Are both pursuing equally successful lives? Is either life being wasted?

Dworkin offered little guidance to help answer these questions. He urged that we "make our lives into works of art,"[3] but works of art typically contain complexities and conflicts not found in the lives of Pat or Lee. The story of each might be told in the form of a play or novel, but neither individual appears to have the makings of a Medea, Hamlet, or Anna Karenina.

Dworkin remarked that "Someone creates a work of art from his life if he lives and loves well in family or community with no fame or artistic achievement at all."[4] Here Dworkin, having urged us to live well by making our lives into works of art, unhelpfully explained that works of art are those made by living well. This circular explanation sheds no light on how to live well, so Dworkin's appeal to works of art does not help us choose between the lives of Pat and Lee.

Many other philosophers, however, have provided reasons for believing that Pat's life is superior to Lee's.[5] They rate the pursuit of philosophical inquiry, playing the cello, or raising a family more highly than surfing, having a series of romances, or living in a luxurious home.

Susan Wolf, for instance, argues that if your life is to have meaning, you need to be engaged with projects of worth, i.e., those with objective (or inherent) value.[6] What are these? Unfortunately, Wolf offers no theory of objective value to guide us, but she does provide examples of activities that are worthwhile and others that are not. For example, she maintains that caring for an ailing friend gives life meaning but providing financial support for a sick stranger does not; practicing a religion gives life meaning but playing computer games does not; climbing a mountain gives life meaning but solving crossword puzzles does not. How about a life devoted exclusively to the practice of corporate law? Is that more akin to climbing a mountain or solving crossword puzzles? Wolf isn't sure and declares the matter controversial. Whether her assessment would be different if the legal specialty were, for example, constitutional law is not clear.

Nevertheless, we might suppose that Wolf would look with greater favor on Pat's interests than Lee's. But perhaps not.

Consider her reply to psychologist Jonathan Haidt, who suspects that Wolf's list of meaningful activities presupposes "*politically liberal* bourgeois American values." As a challenge to her views, he presents the case of one of his students, a shy woman who was passionate about horses: riding them, studying their history, and making "horse friends" with others who shared her passion. Haidt argues that this woman found meaning in life through her interest in horses, but he recognizes that "all of her horsing around does nothing for anyone else, and it does not make the world a better place."[7] Hence according to Haidt, Wolf's theory of objective value fails in this case.

In replying to Haidt, however, Wolf takes a surprising step. Rather than dismissing horses as an appropriate subject on which to build a worthwhile life, Wolf emphasizes that you need not accept someone else's word for what has objective value, then suggests that horses might well contribute to the meaningfulness of the woman's life, and concludes that a person's liking some activity, whatever it may be, can lead to its becoming valuable for that individual. What, then, becomes of objective value? Wolf senses the problem and admits that her discussion "may leave others either disappointed by what they see as watering down of what is distinctive about my conception of meaningfulness, or confused about what the point of it is, if it is to be understood so broadly."[8] We share such confusion.

If we follow Wolf's line of reasoning about the case of the woman who loved horses, then perhaps Lee's life might be on a par with Pat's. After all, if riding horses makes a life worthwhile, why not swimming, driving luxury cars, and traveling to far-flung locations?

Perhaps Wolf goes astray in formulating her list of worthwhile activities, so let us consider the list offered by Richard Kraut, who maintains that "a flourishing human being is one who possesses, develops, and enjoys the exercise of cognitive, affective, sensory, and social powers (no less than physical powers)."[9] Does this description fit Pat better than Lee?

Kraut probably would suppose so, but the answer is not obvious. Consider the following activities he cites with approval: playing tennis, writing poetry, cooking, running an organization, philosophizing, and enjoying our sexual powers. Here are some other activities Kraut finds of lesser value: bowling, playing checkers, accumulating wealth, achieving fame, holding socially isolating jobs, and remaining single.

As with Wolf's list, Kraut's raises more questions than it answers. Why is tennis better than bowling? How do both compare to badminton, archery, or quoits? Why is cooking better than checkers? How do both compare to gardening, hiking, or playing Monopoly? What's the matter with socially isolating jobs, such as serving as a lighthouse keeper, exploring a rain forest, writing fiction in a remote cabin, or doing research in a library cubicle? Why are fame and wealth denigrated, when many of us, including philosophy professors, are motivated by the possibility of receiving increased recognition and higher salaries? Furthermore, why does the study of philosophy invariably appear on philosophers' lists of worthwhile activities, whereas the study of such subjects as sociology, geology, Asian religions, ceramics, and finance are rarely cited with enthusiasm?

Perhaps surprisingly, Kraut's criteria for flourishing might well fit Lee's life: Lee's surfing would presumably lead to greater development of physical powers, Lee's travel might offer a wider perspective on understanding the world, Lee's many friends might offer a richer social life, and Lee's romances might lead to significant development of affective and sexual powers. How are we to weigh these advantages against Pat's devotion to research, teaching, family, and hobbies? The answer is unclear, but if Kraut's criteria do not favor the life of Pat or Lee, what guidance do they provide for living well? In any case, they would be especially unconvincing to an unmarried person who belongs to a bowling league.

Assuming that lists of more and less worthwhile activities offer too easy a target for criticism, why not avoid specifics and simply assert that living well is pursuing goals of intrinsic value? That strategy is adopted by Stephen Darwall, who claims that "the best life for human beings is one of significant engagement in activities through which we come into appreciative rapport with agent-neutral values, such as aesthetic beauty, knowledge and understanding, and the worth of living beings."[10] Darwall here fails to take into account John Dewey's insight that any subject can have intrinsic value. In Dewey's words, "We may imagine a man who at one time thoroughly enjoys converse with his friends; at another the hearing of a symphony; at another the eating of his meals; at another the reading of a book; at another the earning of money; and so on. As an appreciative realization, each of these is an intrinsic value. It occupies a particular place in life; it serves its own end, which cannot be supplied by a substitute."[11] Thus sometimes Pat considers philosophy, bridge, or playing the cello to have intrinsic value, while Lee may think the same of surfing, golf, or travel.

Darwall, however, adds that our activities are meritorious only if others recognize them as such. We should, therefore, focus on "things that matter,"[12] and things matter only if others who care about us judge that our choices have "worth."[13] Do Pat's friends find Pat's life to be of worth? Quite likely. Do Lee's friends find Lee's life to be of worth? Also quite likely. Thus we have reached an impasse.

To illustrate the problem more vividly, consider the real-life case of Phil Saltman, a jazz pianist in the 1930s and 1940s, whose extraordinary talents could have propelled him to international renown.[14] But after appearing as soloist with the Boston Pops Orchestra, he decided that life as a touring musician was not to his liking, and he chose instead to open a summer music camp for boys and girls who enjoyed playing music, even if they did not plan to pursue the activity professionally. The camp flourished,[15] and he never doubted his choice to give up the opportunity for a distinguished solo career in order to guide youngsters and play music with them in amateur combos. Did he make a mistake? Did he limit his chances for a successful life? Did he waste his most significant talents? Some of his friends thought so; others did not. Therefore Darwall's test is unhelpful. Regardless, why should Phil Saltman's friends have been given the final say? They probably did not fully understand his situation, and in any case the life at stake was his, not theirs.

We should also note that like Wolf and Kraut, Darwall takes philosophy as a paradigm case of a worthwhile activity. As he puts it, "Readers of this essay might agree that philosophy and philosophical activity have intrinsic worth."[16]

No doubt most would. Keep in mind, however, the insightful words of the pre-Socratic philosopher Xenophanes (c. 570–478 BCE), who is said to have remarked that "if oxen and horses and lions had hands, and could draw with their hands and do what man can do, horses would draw the gods in the shape of horses, and oxen in the shape of oxen, each giving the gods bodies similar to their own."[17] Of course, most philosophers find philosophy to be worthwhile, just as most chess players find chess to be worthwhile. After all, how many of us suppose that a successful life depends on engaging in activities that we do not enjoy or may hardly understand? Instead, we are prone to urge others to recognize the worth of at least some of our preferred undertakings. For instance, rarely do philosophers fight fires, achieve extraordinary feats of athleticism, or amass large sums of money in business ventures. Few philosophers, therefore, are apt to find as much value in firefighting, professional sports, or commerce as in contemplation.

Now let us return to assessing the lives of Pat and Lee. While we reject the assumption that for all people at all times certain activities are intrinsically more worthy than others, we nevertheless note two crucial ways in which Pat and Lee are alike. Despite the vast differences in their interests, both act morally, neither harming anyone. How could they be living well while behaving unethically?

But Pat and Lee not only act ethically; both are also happy. They have found deep satisfaction in their respective lives. Granted, we might urge either one to consider alternatives. Perhaps we could suggest to Lee the study of philosophy, lauding its power to help understand the human condition. Lee might take our suggestion and find philosophy fascinating; then again, Lee might find it opaque and boring. Likewise, perhaps we could urge Pat to take up golf. Pat might enjoy it, or, contrary to our expectations, consider it a waste of time. We can offer such suggestions to both of them, but doing so doesn't imply that the life of either is in any way unsatisfactory.

Suppose, however, that Pat and Lee were fundamentally frustrated or angry. Suppose they regretted many important decisions they had made, resented how they were treated by others, or rued what they considered to be a long series of misfortunes. Under those circumstances, we do not believe they have achieved well-being. Our view, then, is that acting morally and finding long-term satisfaction are necessary conditions for living well. Seeing no plausible case for any other, we consider them, taken together, to be sufficient. By that standard, Pat and Lee both are living well. We might admire the life of one more than the other, but such a judgment would reflect our own preferences or purposes and not provide an appropriate basis for determining whose life is well-lived.

Notes

1 Ronald Dworkin, *Religion without God* (Cambridge, MA: Harvard University Press, 2013), 155.

2 Dworkin, 114.

3 Dworkin, 157–58.

4 Dworkin, 158.

5 See, for example, Stephen Darwall, *Welfare and Rational Care* (Princeton: Princeton University Press, 2002); Richard Kraut, *What Is Good and Why* (Cambridge, MA: Harvard University Press, 2007); and Susan Wolf, *Meaning in Life and Why It Matters* (Princeton, NJ: Princeton University Press, 2010).

6 Wolf, 34–39.

7 Jonathan Haidt, "Comment" in Wolf, 97.

8 Wolf, 131.

9 Kraut, 137.

10 Darwall, 75.

11 *The Middle Works of John Dewey*, 1899–1924, vol. 9, ed. Jo Ann Boydston (Carbondale: Southern Illinois University Press, 1985), 247.

12 Darwall, 95.

13 Darwall, 97.

14 See his *Method of Modern Jazz Piano Playing*, rev. ed., Boston Music Company, 1937.

15 Known as Camp Encore/Coda, it continues under the directorship of Phil Saltman's son and daughter-in-law; its history can be found at www.encore-coda.com.

16 Darwall, 79.

17 John Manley Robinson, *An Introduction to Early Greek Philosophy* (Boston: Houghton Mifflin Company, 1968).

13
Choosing the Experience Machine

Does the value of happiness depend on how it is achieved? Suppose someone could be made happy by having illusory experiences. Would such happiness be worth choosing? Many believe not, but a different view is defended by me and Christine Vitrano, with whom I coauthored an earlier version of this chapter.

In a frequently cited and widely admired thought experiment, Robert Nozick (1938–2002) offered the following hypothetical: Suppose there were an experience machine that would give you any experience you desired. Super-duper neuropsychologists could stimulate your brain so that you would think and feel you were writing a great novel, or making a friend, or reading an interesting book. All the time you would be floating in a tank, with electrodes attached to your brain. Would you plug in?[1] Nozick presumed that no one would choose this option, and offered three reasons. First, "we want to *do* certain things, and not just have the experience of doing them." Second, "we want to *be* a certain way, to be a certain sort of person." Third, "plugging in ... limits us to a man-made reality." Nozick concluded that because we would not use an experience machine, "something matters to us in addition to experience."[2]

In the decades since Nozick posed the puzzle and presented his solution, most commentators have taken his treatment as conclusive. Almost no one has argued that people would choose the experience machine.

To find such unanimity among philosophers is unexpected, but the situation is especially surprising because Nozick's conclusion appears to us to be mistaken. In support of our view, we shall offer various reasons why an individual might be inclined to choose the experience machine. We illustrate these reasons by the use of numerous examples at least as plausible as the experience machine itself.

First, consider cases in which people may not desire to *do* certain things but instead want to have the experience of doing them. For example, one of the pleasures of going to the movies is having the opportunity to experience adventures we would not risk in reality. While safe in our plush seats, we can feel the excitement of skiing precipitously down a steep mountain, participating in dangerous international intrigue, or battling a typhoon. Yet how many of us actually wish to *do* any of these things? Such cases demonstrate that using an experience machine is not in principle objectionable. The only controversial issue is the length of time for which you would be willing to employ it.

The cinema, however, is not the only case in which we seek appearance rather than reality. Consider the popularity of bungee jumping, roller coasters, aggressive computer games, or re-enacting Civil War battles. All these activities offer participants the experience of pursuing adventures without facing the real-life activities they simulate.

Another sort of escape from reality is offered by psychedelic drugs. Nozick noted that these are viewed by some "as mere local experience machines,"[3] but he did not draw the obvious inference that their widespread use suggests that many would welcome the opportunity not only to drop out but also to plug in. A similar point could be made about the widespread use of alcohol to distort reality.

Granted, the examples we have discussed so far involve individuals who might use the machine only occasionally. And in a later discussion Nozick reformulated his challenge: "The question is not whether to try the machine temporarily, but whether to enter it for the rest of your life."[4]

In response, let us turn to cases in which people, to change who they are, might choose the experience machine for the rest of their lives. Consider golf enthusiasts who struggle to master this most intractable of games. Doing so at a professional level necessitates spending innumerable hours hitting thousands of golf balls day after day over a period of at least a decade. Not many of us would choose to spend our lives in such tiresome training (even if we had the potential to excel, as most of us do not). Suppose, however, that without any preparation you could experience hitting massive drives, pinpoint iron shots, and precision putts, while hearing the roars of the crowd as you win major championships. Wouldn't many amateur golfers want that life? Wouldn't they be willing to trade their frustration on the fairways for a life of golfing triumphs?

Or consider the ardent music lover who dreams of becoming a concert pianist. Few persons, even if they had the necessary talent, would choose to exhaust their energy and patience in such a strenuous effort. But suppose that without any exertion they could have the experience of performing recitals in great halls and appearing as soloist with the world's leading symphony orchestras, each time receiving adulation from a cheering audience. Might some not be willing to trade their lives in order to undergo such experiences?

Imagine that instead of living your own life, you could choose to live the life of Alexander the Great, Cleopatra, or Babe Ruth. Do you suppose no one would willingly make that trade, even though the experience machine could be programmed to omit a life's tribulations and focus on its triumphs? Or how about living the life of secret agent James Bond? Wouldn't that option tempt some?

Another sort of case concerns individuals who would wish to change their characters. For example, how would you feel if you possessed the moral and intellectual virtues of the Buddha? The experience machine could provide the answer.

Or suppose you wish to have been present at the trial of Socrates, the Lincoln-Douglas debates, or the riot at the Paris premiere of Stravinsky's *Le Sacre du printemps*. The experience machine could make you a spectator at those events. Of course, you wouldn't actually be there. Your experience, however, would be indistinguishable from reality.

The experience machine would also enable you to have experiences of inestimable personal value. For example, you could experience a world inhabited by your loved ones who have died. In our dreams we often imagine such a scenario and, when awakened, are disappointed the dream did not continue. Suppose, however, you could opt for the vision to endure. Wouldn't many do so?

Similarly, the experience machine would enable you to return to a happier time in your life. Wouldn't many people want to make that trip into the past?

Another reason why people might choose the experience machine is a desire to escape a life of sorrow or even agony. Nozick, when revisiting the idea of the experience machine, declared such cases irrelevant, perhaps because he presumed that they occur infrequently.[5] The truth, however, is otherwise. The plight of so many unfortunate people is captured in this verse of William Blake:

> Every Night & every Morn
> Some to Misery are Born.
> Every Morn & every Night
> Some are Born to sweet delight.
> Some are Born to sweet delight,
> Some are Born to Endless Night.[6]

Those born in the latter circumstance would surely choose the delights of the experience machine in place of their dreadful lives on earth.

How many unfortunate souls are in this position? Consider the view of Arthur Schopenhauer (1788–1860):

> Life with its hourly, daily, weekly, yearly, little, greater, and great misfortunes, with its deluded hopes and its accidents destroying all our calculations, bears so distinctly the impression of

> something with which we must become disgusted, that it is hard to conceive how one has been able to mistake this and allow oneself to be persuaded that life is there in order to be thankfully enjoyed, and that man exists in order to be happy.[7]

One need not be as pessimistic as Schopenhauer to sympathize with his outlook. If the experience machine offers joys in place of tortures of mind and body, the burden of argument would surely rest on those who would urge against its use.

After all, we avoid the pain of surgery by the use of anesthesia; we thereby avoid reality. If one's life itself is little more than a succession of pains, why not opt, instead, for the delights of the experience machine?

Nozick asserted that "plugging into the machine is a kind of suicide."[8] He said, however, that the machine enables one to choose a "lifetime of bliss."[9] Hence wouldn't plugging in be the closest we could come to heaven on earth? After all, what is heaven supposed to be if not eternal bliss?

Nozick concluded that we desire to be "in contact with reality."[10] Knowing what we do of reality, however, why assume that remaining in touch with it is invariably preferable to a lifetime of bliss?

We believe that the array of cases we have presented demonstrates the implausibility of the assumption that no one would use the experience machine. Indeed, were such a machine on the market, a shrewd investor would seek to purchase it, or at least buy stock in the company that manufactured it.

But what lessons were we supposed to learn from the claim that no one would choose the machine? Jonathan Glover believes Nozick's thought experiment demonstrates that "we care about more than our own experiences."[11] No doubt some of us do, and some of us don't. We shouldn't, however, confuse caring about something with being unwilling to trade it under appropriate circumstances. Epidural anesthesia is chosen by many women to ease the pain of labor and delivery, but doing so does not imply that they devalue the reality of childbirth. Similarly, choosing to plug into the experience machine does not imply a lack of concern for reality. Such concern may simply be overridden.

James Griffin presumes that rejecting the experience machine demonstrates that knowing the truth rather than being comforted by delusions makes for "a better life."[12] That conclusion is easier to reach, however, if one's life is satisfying. But for those suffering in "endless night," the value of delusions should not be so quickly dismissed. In any case, would you want to know the truth regarding the time and circumstances of your death? Indeed, grasping more of the truth does not always lead to a better life. Who would want to know the deepest thoughts of all others? The truth matters, but it may be traded for something more valuable.

Nozick believed that we value reality over the mere experience of it. As our cases appear to demonstrate, however, sometimes we don't value reality highly, or even at all. As Hume in his *Dialogues Concerning Natural Religion* puts the point in the mouth of the orthodox believer Demea:

> The whole earth ... is cursed and polluted. A perpetual war is kindled amongst all living creatures. Necessity, hunger, want stimulate the strong and courageous; fear, anxiety, terror agitate the weak and infirm. The first entrance into life gives anguish to the new-born infant and to its wretched parent; weakness, impotence, distress attend each stage of that life, and it is, at last, finished in agony and horror.[13]

Such is our world, and for good reason some would wish to explore other possibilities. They may still value aspects of reality but would be willing to trade them for something they believe more valuable. Whether such exchanges would be wise depends on the circumstances. To suppose, however, that, regardless of the attractiveness of the alternatives, such a choice would never be made seems unwarranted. Once that error is recognized, Nozick's experience machine can be seen as what it is: a dream for which many may yearn but not evidence that mere experience is insufficient for happiness.

Notes

1 Robert Nozick, *Anarchy, State, and Utopia* (New York: Basic Books, Inc., 1974), 42–43.

2 Nozick, 43.

3 Nozick, 44.

4 Robert Nozick, *The Examined Life: Philosophical Meditations* (New York: Simon & Schuster, 1990), 105.

5 *The Examined Life*, 105.

6 William Blake, "Auguries of Innocence," in *William Blake: The Complete Poems*, ed. Alicia Ostriker (London and New York: Penguin, 2004), 510.

7 Arthur Schopenhauer, "On the Variety and Suffering of Life," in Steven M. Cahn and Christine Vitrano, eds., *Happiness: Classic and Contemporary Readings in Philosophy* (New York and Oxford: Oxford University Press), 115.

8 *Anarchy, State, and Utopia*, 43.

9 Ibid., 43.

10 Ibid., 45.

11 Jonathan Glover, *What Sort of People Should There Be?* (New York: Penguin Books, 1984), 285.

12 James Griffin, *Well-Being* (Oxford: Oxford University Press, 2011), 9.

13 David Hume, *Dialogues Concerning Natural Religion and Other Writings*, pt. 10, par. 8.

PART VI: SOCIETY

14
The Case for Democracy

Political philosophy explores the nature and justification of government. A central issue is the relative advantages or disadvantages of democracy (rule by all), monarchy (rule by one), or oligarchy (rule by a few). Some might suppose that the case for democracy is obvious, but matters are not so simple.

Consider the following scenario. On election day you go to a polling place where, waiting to cast ballots, are various members of the community—a carpenter, a gardener, a lawyer, a bus driver, a piano tuner, and an artist. Each has one vote, and the will of the majority prevails.

Standing in line, we might imagine, is Archie Bunker, the engaging but ill-informed and bigoted figure in the classic television sitcom *All in the Family*. Were Archie asked about his preferences, he might reply that he has no idea who is running in this election, but it makes no difference to him, because he has voted for the same party his entire life and has no intention of ever switching. As for the bond issue that appears on the upper right-hand corner of the voting machine, he hadn't realized it was there, but now that you mentioned it, he will be sure to vote against it, because he votes against all bond issues as a waste of money. (If Archie strikes you as a caricature, remember that politicians always seek to place their names at the top of the ballot, because a sizable number of voters automatically select whichever name is first.)

Standing behind Archie is a professor of political science who has devoted her life to a study of the country's political system. She may be familiar with the views of every candidate and even have helped formulate the exact wording of the bond issue. Yet, like Archie, she receives only one vote; her erudition entitles her to nothing more.

Does this arrangement make sense? After all, if you visit a physician seeking advice as to whether to undergo an operation, you would be appalled if the doctor explained that the policy in that office was to poll a random sample of passersby and act in accordance with the will of the majority. A community would be similarly dismayed if it hired an engineer to build a bridge, and the engineer announced that deciding how deeply to lay the foundations would be decided by a vote of the townspeople. In short, to deal with medical or engineering problems, we seek expert judgment, not the uniformed opinions of the populace. Why, then, faced with political problems, do we take the issue to all the people rather than to specialists?

More than two millennia ago Plato considered this same question in his monumental dialogue, *The Republic*. Believing no answer to be reasonable, he developed a system of government based on the view that issues of public policy, being complex, technical matters, ought to be placed in the hands of experts. This Platonic utopia was to be ruled by a small group of philosopher-kings, chosen on the basis of their aptitudes and educated for their roles. Most members of society were to be tradespeople: the farmer was expected only to farm, the cobbler only to cobble. They were to play no role in the governance of the state, and their education was to be in the narrowest sense a trade education.

Indeed, from Plato's viewpoint, even to suggest that farmers or cobblers should participate in the affairs of government would have been a serious mistake, for the farmer was fitted only to farm, the cobbler fitted only to cobble. The philosopher-kings were fitted to rule, and they would do so most effectively if not interfered with by those ill-suited to deliberate about decisions affecting the future of their society.

Plato compared the workings of a democratic society to the situation aboard a ship on which the sailors are arguing over the control of the helm, while none has ever learned navigation.[1] If someone happens to possess needed skills, that person's qualifications will be disregarded on the grounds that steering a ship requires no special competence. Plato scornfully observed that "with a magnificent indifference to the sort of life a person has led before he enters politics ... [a democracy] will promote to honor anyone who merely calls himself the people's friend."[2]

To ensure that those who will serve as philosopher-kings are qualified to take on their responsibilities, Plato required that prospective office-holders embark on a rigorous intellectual program, topped off by the study of dialectic, that is, analyzing key concepts in the light of a vision of the good. No doubt many today would be more inclined to concentrate such advanced education for political leadership less on the intricacies of abstract reasoning and more on issues in political science, economics, sociology, and international relations. The force of Plato's proposal, however, is not found in the specifics of the curriculum he proposed but in the notion that office-holders should be required to receive intellectual preparation for their positions.

In defense of democracy, however, we should remember that by whatever procedures the rulers of an aristocracy such as Plato's may be selected, mistakes are possible, and as the events of history have so often demonstrated, once unrestrained authority is placed in the wrong hands, the results are likely to be calamitous. In a democracy, a foolish decision made on one occasion can be undone on another, but when all control has been transferred to the aristocrats, second chances are no longer possible. Members of a democracy avoid having to make the difficult, dangerous, and unalterable decision of whom to entrust with unrestricted power.

Furthermore, even if the rulers are initially kindhearted, in time they tend to lose touch with the ruled. Even the best-intentioned sovereigns may find difficulty remaining sensitive to the needs and desires of those under their control.

Although an elite may possess greater expertise in certain technical matters than do other individuals, members of a society possess special insight into their own problems, interests, and goals. As Dewey pointed out, "the individuals of the submerged mass may not be very wise. But there is one thing they are wiser about than anybody else can be, and that is where the shoe pinches, the troubles they suffer from."[3] Only the democratic system ensures that this self-knowledge is taken into account in the governmental process.

A democratic society, moreover, is distinguished by the quality of life inherent in its procedures. Competitive elections require the expression of opposing points of view, and the protection of the right of all citizens to speak freely, write freely, and assemble freely, thus producing a vitality that enriches all. For such reasons, Winston Churchill (1874–1965), although recognizing the weaknesses of democracy, described it as the worst form of government except for all the others that have been tried.

Surprisingly, Plato agreed, but he expressed that view not in *The Republic* but in what is widely thought to be a later dialogue, namely, *The Statesman*.[4] There, near the end of the work, Plato compared three types of government: monarchy, the rule of one; aristocracy, the rule of a few; and democracy, the rule of all.

Plato maintained that if the monarch is ideal, possessing moral and intellectual insight and treating all persons fairly, then monarchy is the best form of government. If, however, the monarch does not govern wisely, then monarchy can degenerate into tyranny, the worst form of government. Similarly, if a small group of rulers always governs wisely, then aristocracy is the second-best form of government. But if the aristocracy does not govern wisely, then it can degenerate into oligarchy, the second worst form of government. According to Plato, the advantage of democracy is that it is capable of no great good or any serious evil. Thus in a society like ours that is not perfectly law-abiding and in which all do not always carry out their responsibilities appropriately, the best form of government, according to Plato, is democracy. Despite its faults, it carries the fewest dangers and hence is the wisest choice.

The case for democracy strikes most as persuasive. Note, however, that it does not rest on democracy's always producing the best results but, instead, avoiding the worst.

Notes

1 *The Republic of Plato*, trans. Francis MacDonald Cornford (New York: Oxford University Press, 1945), 488b–489.

2 Plato, 558b.

3 John Dewey, "Democracy," in Steven M. Cahn, ed., *Exploring Philosophy*, 6th ed. (New York: Oxford University Press, 2018), 484.

4 Plato, *Statesman*, trans. Christopher J. Rowe (Indianapolis: Hackett Publishing Company, 1999), 291d–303b.

15

The Content of Liberal Education

How can the members of a democracy be provided with the understanding and capability to reap the greatest possible benefits from the democratic process while protecting it from those who would undermine it? A key is found in the enterprise of liberal education.

In a democracy every citizen's education should be of concern, for the ignorance of some is a threat to all. Yet some critics of higher education have complained that it wastes resources on many better suited only for job training. This objection, however, misunderstands the nature of a democratic society. After all, how can the electorate be too educated, how can they know too much, and how can they be too astute? Too little education, however, and democracy becomes vulnerable to intellectual chicanery and moral vacuity.

But what knowledge, skills, and values are necessary for individuals to live intelligently and responsibly as free persons in a free society?

In addition to possessing an understanding of the democratic system itself, every member of a democracy should be able to read, write, and speak effectively so as to be able to participate fully in the free exchange of ideas that is vital to an open society. Every member of a democracy should also be able to comprehend the range of public issues, from poverty, climate change, and ideological conflict, to the dangers of nuclear warfare and the benefits of space research. These topics cannot be intelligently discussed by those ignorant of the physical structure of the world, the forces that shape society, or the ideas and events that form the background of present crises. Thus every member of a democracy should possess substantial knowledge of physical science, social science, world history, and national history.

The study of science assumes familiarity with the fundamental concepts and techniques of mathematics, because such notions play a critical role in the physical sciences and an ever-increasing role in the social sciences. Furthermore, to know only the results of scientific and historical investigations is not sufficient; one needs also to understand the methods of inquiry that have produced these results. No amount of knowledge brings intellectual sophistication, unless one also possesses the power of critical thinking. Therefore every member of a democracy should be familiar with the canons of logic and scientific method.

Still another characteristic that should be common to all members of a democracy is sensitivity to aesthetic experience. An appreciation of literature, art, and music enriches the imagination, refines the sensibilities, and provides increased awareness of our world. In a society of aesthetic illiterates, not only the quality of art suffers but also the quality of life.

In connection with literature, note that significant value is derived from reading foreign literature in its original language. Not only does great literature lose some of its richness in translation, but learning another language increases linguistic sensitivity and makes one more conscious of the unique potentialities and limitations of any particular tongue. Such study is also a most effective means of widening cultural horizons, for understanding another language is a key to understanding another culture.

Every member of a democracy should also acquire intellectual perspective, the ability to scrutinize the fundamental principles of thought and action, encompassing both what is and what ought to be. The path to such wisdom lies in the study of those subtle analyses and grand visions that comprise philosophy. No other subject affords a stronger defense against intimidation by dogmatism while simultaneously providing a framework for the operation of intelligence.

An education that contains these elements is known as a *liberal education.* It can be summarized, in the words of Sidney Hook (1902–89), as including "selected materials from the fields of mathematics and the natural sciences; social studies, including history; language and literature; philosophy and logic; art and music. The knowledge imparted by such study should be acquired in such a way as to strengthen the skills of reading and writing, of thinking and imaginative interpretation, of criticism and evaluation."[1] Such an education requires that students go beyond their vocational interests and be equipped with sufficient understanding and capability to fulfill their responsibilities as informed citizens. Thus does the success of a democracy depend on a broad education that contributes to a vigorous and enlightened society.

Note

1 Sidney Hook, *Education for Modern Man: A New Perspective* (New York: Alfred A. Knopf, 1963), 155.

About the Author

Steven M. Cahn is Professor Emeritus of Philosophy at the City University of New York Graduate Center, where he served for nearly a decade as Provost and Vice President for Academic Affairs, then as Acting President.

He was born in Springfield, Massachusetts, in 1942. After earning an AB from Columbia College in 1963 and PhD in philosophy from Columbia University in 1966, Dr. Cahn taught at Dartmouth College, Vassar College, New York University, the University of Rochester, and the University of Vermont, where he chaired the Department of Philosophy.

He then served as a program officer at the Exxon Education Foundation, as Acting Director for Humanities at the Rockefeller Foundation, and as the first Director of General Programs at the National Endowment for the Humanities. He formerly chaired the American Philosophical Association's Committee on the Teaching of Philosophy, was the Association's delegate to the American Council of Learned Societies, and was longtime President of the John Dewey Foundation.

Dr. Cahn is the author of sixteen books, including *Fate, Logic, and Time*; *Saints and Scamps: Ethics in Academia, 25th Anniversary Edition*; *From Student to Scholar: A Candid Guide to Becoming a Professor*; *Happiness and Goodness: Philosophical Reflections on Living Well* (with Christine Vitrano); *Polishing Your Prose* (with Victor L. Cahn); *Religion within Reason*; *Teaching Philosophy: A Guide*; and *Inside Academia: Professors, Politics, and Policies.*

He has edited or coedited nearly fifty books, including *The World of Philosophy*, now in its second edition; *Exploring Philosophy of Religion*, now in its second edition; *Classic and Contemporary Readings in the Philosophy of Education*, now in its second edition; *Political Philosophy*, now in its third edition; *Exploring Ethics*, now in its fifth edition; *Exploring Philosophy*, now in its sixth edition; and *Classics of Western Philosophy*, now in its eighth edition.

A collection of essays written in his honor, edited by two of his former doctoral students, Robert B. Talisse of Vanderbilt University and Maureen Eckert of the University of Massachusetts Dartmouth, is titled *A Teacher's Life: Essays for Steven M. Cahn.*

Permissions Acknowledgments

Chapter 3 adapted from "Dummy Hypotheses," Chapter 6 of *Religion within Reason* by Steven M. Cahn. Copyright © 2002 Columbia University Press. Reprinted with the permission of Columbia University Press.

Chapter 5 adapted from "Random Choices," in *Philosophy and Phenomenological Research* 37.4 (June 1977): 549–51.

Chapter 7 adapted from "The Theodicy Trap," in *Think* 15.44 (2016): 23–28.

Chapter 8 adapted from "The Irrelevance to Religion of Philosophic Proofs for the Existence of God," from the *American Philosophical Quarterly* 6.3 (1969). Used with the permission of Dr. Nicholas Rescher.

Chapter 11, Part A adapted from "The Bus Puzzle," in *Teaching Ethics* 15:2 (2015).

Index

From the Publisher

A name never says it all, but the word "Broadview" expresses a good deal of the philosophy behind our company. We are open to a broad range of academic approaches and political viewpoints. We pay attention to the broad impact book publishing and book printing has in the wider world; for some years now we have used 100% recycled paper for most titles. Our publishing program is internationally oriented and broad-ranging. Our individual titles often appeal to a broad readership too; many are of interest as much to general readers as to academics and students.

Founded in 1985, Broadview remains a fully independent company owned by its shareholders—not an imprint or subsidiary of a larger multinational.

For the most accurate information on our books (including information on pricing, editions, and formats) please visit our website at www.broadviewpress.com. Our print books and ebooks are available for sale on our site.

broadview press

www.broadviewpress.com

This book is made of paper from well-managed FSC® - certified forests, recycled materials, and other controlled sources.